PRAISE FOR RACHAEL HERRON

On *Fast-Draft Your Memoir:*

“Simply put, if you have ever struggled to finish a book, if you have a yen to write about a time in your life, but aren't sure how to structure it, where to start, how to get through the middle and across the finish line---THIS BOOK IS FOR YOU.”

- Barbara Edelman

With the help of Herron’s advice, a person can stop careening across the writing highway, make forward progress between the lines, and successfully complete the first draft of a memoir.

- Kristine Kay Mieztner

Fiction:

“A poignant, profound ode to the enduring and redemptive power of love.” – Library Journal

"A celebration of the power of love to heal even the most broken of hearts." - NYT Bestselling Author Susan Wiggs

“A heart-warming story of family, friendship and love in a town you’ll never want to leave.” – Barbara Freethy, USA Today Bestseller

ALSO BY RACHAEL HERRON

Standalone novels:

The Ones Who Matter Most

Splinters of Light

Pack Up the Moon

The Darling Bay Novels

The Darling Songbirds

The Songbird's Call

The Songbird Sisters

Cypress Hollow Novels:

How to Knit a Love Song

How to Knit a Heart Back Home

Wishes & Stitches

Cora's Heart

Fiona's Flame

Memoir:

A Life in Stitches

Nonfiction:

Fast-Draft Your Memoir: Write Your Life Story in 45 Hours

ONWARD, WRITER!

29 Encouraging Letters to Your Inner Writer

RACHAEL HERRON

Hga

ISBN: 978-1-940785-40-0

HGA Publishing

INTRODUCTION

Hello, writer!

A while back, I decided that when it came to my writing, I needed some ass-kicking mixed with some gentle kindness. I've found plenty of both in separate places out there in Writing Book-Landia, but it's hard to find that particular *mix* in just one book. And if there's a writing book out there, you be can be sure I've either got it on my bookshelf or in my Kindle. I'm kind of addicted to them.

I find writers are a curious breed in that we pretend as if we live in the real world, but really, we don't. In the back of our brains (or sometimes right up in the front), we're always thinking about writing. We might *look* like we're listening to you, but honestly, we're jotting down mental notes about the way your voice sounds so that we can steal it later to use in our work, or worse, we've tuned out completely and are actually just thinking about the next time we can get back to the page and quit beating ourselves up for taking so long to finish chapter seven.

Writers, when they go away on vacation together, talk about almost nothing but writing. We never, ever get tired of talking about it. When we're together in the bar at a conference, the conversation doesn't wander very often to politics or family—we talk nonstop about craft, industry gossip, writing mindset, and the very *how* of getting our writing done. We exchange agent names, we swap editor stories, we share how we're going to publicize the next book, and how that might change the writing game for us.

We just want to write (though, honestly, it's the hardest thing to do of all), and if we're not doing that, we want to be reading or talking about writing.

So welcome to my letters. I send them to my writing group, but honestly, I write them for myself. I have bad writing days—oh, so many of them—and I write these so that I can remind myself that yes, I'm all right. It's okay to forgive myself. And it's okay to encourage myself and to give myself tough love and follow it with a compassionate scoop of chocolate peanut butter ice cream.

But who am I to tell you all this?

I got my Masters of Fine Arts in Creative Writing at Mills College. I've written more than twenty books, which include mainstream literary fiction, memoir, and feminist romance. I teach writing in the extension programs at UC Berkeley and Stanford. I've been lucky enough to have taught writing around the world, but my favorite place to teach is from the chair I'm in at this very moment. I have my feet up on my beat-up rolltop desk and a dog or two snoring on the divan behind me.

I think writing is the best job in the whole world. It took me ten years of active writing to get to the point where I could leave my day job and pursue writing full-time, and I never take a single day in this chair for granted.

I also think writing isn't something we should attempt alone. As writers, we have to move through our pages by ourselves, but we need to come up for air sometimes. We need a water cooler to lean against, we need to know that our comrades-in-arms understand what we're going through. We need community and support. That's what these letters are meant to be for you. These short chapters include every aspect of my personality. Some are liberal in their leaning (I believe writers should speak their minds). I swear a little bit, but not nearly as much as I do in person (I believe writers should use *all* the words they can get their hands on). They're very much *me,* a bit frantic, a little manic, a lot happy, sometimes despairing, and always (always) hopeful.

Happy writing to you.

Onward!

xo,

Rachael

CHAPTER ONE

This Is for When You're a Good Writer

Hi writer friends,

I just heard writer Rebecca Hunter say something that I really related with. I mean I *just* heard her, about an hour ago. I rushed home to write this letter (and to take a nap, but that's for after I hit send on this).

She was talking about how she'd made a goal for herself to finish a book before she was forty. She hadn't yet (at that point), because: **"I was waiting to write until I became a good writer. That strategy? Yeah, it didn't work out that well."**

Rebecca finally realized that she would never get better without actually writing. She wrote a book. Then multiple books. She wrote and kept writing.

See, most of us come with some built-in talent. If you're reading this, I bet you have it, too. People have told us we're fantastic with words. Why, then, is it so *hard* to actually do the work? We'd better wait till we learn some more—maybe then we'll be able to figure out how.

I was this way, completely.

I read all the writing books.

I talked to all the writers.

I thought really really *really* hard about what I was going to write someday.

I wrote sentences (glorious ones! Ones that could light the world on fire!) in my head while I did dishes.

I thought up new plots while I was driving.

But I never did the work, because I was waiting for that magical day when I would wake up a better writer.

The bad news: That day won't come unless you're writing.

How do you write when you don't feel ready?

My darling, you just do. You write a crappy first paragraph. You follow that with a crappy first page. Then comes the crappy first scene, then the crappy first chapter. Soon enough? You have a terrible book! You *let* yourself write terrible, awful dreck because it is better than not writing. You're learning while you're writing crappily.

The good news: There are bright, sparkling, magically wonderful words in that draft. You probably won't see them when you write them. It's when you're sifting through the pages later that you'll stumble on something brilliant, something tinged with filigreed gold at its edges.

You'll find words that string together like twinkle lights, words that sing like garden fairies on a champagne bender.

And from *there* you move forward.

In the memoir class I taught this semester, I asked the students to write the last chapter of their books midway through class. One writer, Susanna, had the revelation I knew someone would have.

"So, I was writing along, enjoying the exercise, and then my subconscious said that maybe part of what I was writing just then might be a better beginning than the new beginning I wrote three months ago. Crud. Was this an evil plot by my writing teacher?"

Hmmm. One wonders, doesn't one?

Being surprised by your own writing is a source of such happiness that it pays for all the dreck we have to push through to get there.

Now, it's not easy. You will suck.

Personally, I'm exceedingly terrible at writing at least five or six times a week. (This might be one of them!) I sincerely mean this—I'm not being fake-modest. For every draft of anything I write (a tweet, a Facebook post, a book), I leap into the air, and I'm never sure I won't land face-first in a mud puddle. I'm getting better at not ending up wet and muddy, but that's because I have heaps of practice.

That said, there's real, true joy to be found in splashing in puddles, isn't there? If you're new to the writing gig, or you still feel like you're waiting to become a better writer before you commit your thoughts to the page, remember: *you're just a kid when it comes to writing.* We all are, no matter how innately talented we are, until we've written at least two or three books.

What that means is you *get* to splash in puddles. You're not *supposed* to be able to keep yourself clean and neat and tidy all the time. That's not how kids learn! Kids learn to walk by falling down. They learn you can't always tell the depth of the puddle by sight. They fall out of trees. Sometimes it kind of hurts. Sometimes it hurts a whole hell of a lot and you hear yourself doing that hiccuped-forever-inhalation that comes before the scream.

But mud can also be fun, if you embrace it.

I'm in Northern California, and it's raining here this weekend. Instead of driving (because we *don't* know how to drive when the air is even slightly damp), I'm going to take the dogs for a wet hike and splash in puddles. Then I'll splash around on the page.

Join me?

Onward!

xo,

Rachael

CHAPTER TWO

On Blogging

Hello, writers!

I'm so excited you're reading this! (I really, *really* am.) I want these missives to be chatty and friendly and short, so you can get back to writing (or lying in bed or feeding the kids or chasing the bus or whatever else you're doing right now).

This week, I'm thinking about the muse and the fact that I actually have one. I didn't know that until today. I walked onto the Mills campus and realized that fall had arrived with a thump, and my heart flew upward.

I *wanted* to write for my blog.

Huh. My muse is tied to my *blog?* I had no idea.

Now, everyone will tell you blogs are dead, but don't believe them. Blogs are where we still go when we're moved to write something that we want to share not only with the readers we have but also with the readers we might *someday* have. And they're where we go to write for *ourselves.* For that reason, I think they're important for writers to have.

Now, they are in no way a must! If you hate the idea of blogging, please don't! No one will mind!

But if you're drawn to blogging at all, or if you used to blog and you've fallen off the bloggety horse, why don't you start it back up?

This is the way I blog:

I blog when the muse comes and tickles my chin, like when I'm walking through fall leaves. Or when I'm really mad about something. Or, honestly, when I want to write down a recipe I've invented so I can find it again years later.

My blog is most of all—I realize this now, and quite late—for me. I used to think it was for current readers. But lately I've been going through old posts, sorting them into Writing posts and Non-Writing ones (there are a *lot* of writing ones), and I realize what I've been writing is a public journal to myself.

To remind myself where I've been and where I want to go.

And thank God for it—I really do have the worst memory in the world. I'm a very good person to tell jokes to because I never, ever, ever remember the punch lines. I'm also an appreciative audience for my own stories later on. "Really? That happened to me? That's hilarious/so sad/awesome/wild!"

So yes, I recommend blogging. Or journaling in any form.

It's not about how many readers come by. It's not about stats.

It's about you, watching yourself write.

Now, friends, onward!

xo,

Rachael

PS—I'm really glad you're here. Did I mention that?

CHAPTER THREE

Breath and Words

Hi writers,

This morning, I was lying on the floor of my office after doing yoga, trying and *completely* failing to think about my breath.

It's such a simple thing. Just counting the breaths as they come and go. It shouldn't be hard. Why is it often so impossible?

I found myself beating myself up about it. *Jeez. You suck at this. You're not good at meditation. You're not good at any kind of relaxing at all, as a matter of fact. You might as well be doing math in your head, except you're not that good at math, either.*

My brain picked up the ball and kept running. *I'm so bad at this it actually reminds me of writing. I* ***think*** *I should be good at writing, and I sit down and instead of writing gorgeous prose, I just SUCK.*

We all feel it, don't we? We sit down with the perfect phrase in mind, but once the words hit the screen, they're just wrong. Or even worse, we have a feeling we want to capture, and instead, the idea falls completely flat. Dead.

Other days are magical and the lines you capture sing like

crystalline fire was poured from the mind of God through your hands and onto the page.

The only way we can sort out the good from the bad, the easy from the difficult, is to just keep feeling it.

It's just important to show up, and to *keep* showing up.

Some days are golden. And other days you end up drenched and freezing, and the hems of your jeans get covered with mud.

I realized this while on my yoga mat: It's the same damn thing.

Being terrible at watching my breath.

Being terrible at getting words on the page.

No big deal. I keep coming back, and incrementally, I get a little better. If anyone had ever told me that it would take one full year of daily yoga to get my heels to hit the mat in downward dog, I would have probably stopped trying. I'm so impatient with everything that it would have just bummed me out.

Instead, I didn't attach any importance to whether my heels hit the mat or not. I just kept showing up (because God knows I spend enough time at my computer. I need to do *one* healthy thing a day). Then one day, my heels hit. Now they're there, on the mat behind me, every day.

I used to be regularly frustrated by being unable to capture my exact thoughts on the page. I told myself, though, that it was okay. I kept writing anyway. One day, I could fix a little of my writing into something I thought was a little better. One day, a while after that, I was able to push my words into a form that I loved.

It takes time.

It takes showing up.

It takes being okay with the fact that we *all* suck when we first start doing the hard things, the things that matter. And then, even after we get a little better at doing them? We still have bad days. Lots of them.

The joy is remembering to breathe again.

The joy is writing more words and watching where our sentences take us.

It's *all* unexpected.

And why yes, I sure did have all these thoughts while on my yoga mat, a place where I should have just been breathing.

And that's okay, too.

Onward!

xo,

Rachael

CHAPTER FOUR

The Writer's Workout

I have lots of tools in my writing toolbox. The intention of this weekly letter is to share them with you, one by one. It's good to have a hammer. Everyone needs one of those. But if you're trying to saw a board, your hammer won't be much use.

The number one tool in my writer's toolbox is meditation.

Whoops! Before you unsubscribe, I *swear* this is not woo-woo. It's scientific (brain scans show meditation improves mental focus). It's secular. No religion was harmed (or called upon) in the making of this letter.

The hardest thing about writing is the thinking, am I right? As a society, we're not used to thinking very hard about one thing for longer than sixty or eighty seconds at a time. When you sit down at the computer to write, or when you pull out your notebook and put pen to paper, one of the greatest challenges is to stay present, to catch those thoughts that dance as randomly as dust motes in sunlight.

Meditation is push-ups for the mind.

I mean it exactly like that. Meditation makes the muscles in your mind stronger, more willing to work, less upset when distractions occur, and more ready to circle back and do a little more work before heading for another cup of coffee.

In the memoir class I'm teaching, I gave the students a grand three-minute meditation explanation. I'm giving you the even more abbreviated version here.

Three simple steps to secular meditation:

1. Sit (or lie down, I don't care—I do both, depending on how I feel). Strict Meditators (I am not one) will tell you not to lie down, lest you fall asleep. But wouldn't that be *nice* if it happened?

2. Think about your breath. (I count to ten to keep myself thinking about it. When I'm suddenly at fourteen, I know I've spaced out. And what I mean by thinking about your breath is just to *notice* it. Every breath is a little bit different. You don't have to breathe deeply or in any certain way, just watch how your lungs fill, how your stomach rises.)

3. Get distracted.

Repeat steps 2 and 3. Start with five minutes a day. Move up to ten, gradually. Then Bob's your uncle—you've got a stronger mind!

That's it. That third step, the distraction one, is the part that freaks people out, that makes them think they're bad at meditation. The fact is, they're not. YOUR BRAIN WILL GET DISTRACTED. Mine does on a split-second basis. Meditation is only this: learning to be okay with getting distracted and gently going back to what you were trying to do.

And that's the writing magic.

Meditation is push-ups for your brain and is directly usable in your writing practice. You may only be able to do a couple of push-ups at first, but if you meditate a tiny bit today, your brain gets stronger. Happier. Literally.

So the next time you go back to the page, you write a sentence, you get distracted, and then? You're a little bit easier on yourself. Your brain is a little bit stronger and at the same time, you're a little bit gentler on yourself. You've done a few of those mental push-ups. You know you can jump right back into writing after wondering how on earth that cat got so fat when you know for a *fact* you don't feed him that much.

That's it. It can't hurt. It can only help. No time? You can do it before you fall asleep (this used to be the only time I could find to practice, and it made sleeping so much better, too).

Push-ups that lead to better sleep? Better writing? That I can do with my eyes closed? They've worked for me. Give 'em a try and tell me what you think?

Onward, friends!

xo,

Rachael

CHAPTER FIVE

Ira Glass's Theory of The Gap

Hi writers!

In my classes, I always talk about Ira Glass's Gap theory (the artistic gap, not the place where you get jeans). It was something that explained a *lot* to me when I was starting out. (Google for the video—it's good.)

As a reader, your taste is killer. You know good writing when you read it. You appreciate it. You drink it like water and you love being near, in, and around it.

But as a writer, perhaps you're not quite there yet. (I know. It hurts. We've *all* felt this way.)

Because of that excellent taste of yours, you can see that what you're making just isn't up to the level you want it to be.

At this point, most writers quit.

Know what closes that gap?

Writing. More writing. Lots and lots and lots of writing. Yes, we learn from reading, from teachers, from craft books, from consciously *thinking* about our writing. But we learn most of all from *doing the work.*

We learn most from putting our butts in the chair and writing badly. Every day we're getting better (this is true—believe it even if you can't feel it yet).

That's the beautiful thing. You don't actually have to *try* to get better (so stop worrying about how to do that). You just get better and better, the more you write. Automatically.

So go write badly. Fix it later, or throw it out—it's served its purpose just by coming out of your fingertips.

Onward!

xo,

Rachael

CHAPTER SIX

Ideas Are Cheap

Hi writers,

I can't *tell* you how many times I've heard "I have a great idea for a book. Buy me a coffee sometime, and I'll tell it to you. Then you can write it and we can split the money."

"No, thanks," I say. It's too hard to explain to them that ideas are the easy part.

"Okay, okay. Just give me ten percent."

"You're so sweet. But that's okay."

"*FINE*. You drive a hard bargain. I'll *give* you this idea, just put my name with yours on the cover. This must be how you got all the other ideas for your books, huh? People give 'em to you?"

I smile as brightly as I can and point toward where I think the restrooms might be. "Just a sec. I'll be right back." (I don't go back.)

At one point, I believed that ideas were the magic of writing, too. That was back when I didn't write much because I was still busy trying to come up with the perfect plot. Once I got the *best* idea in my mind, I knew the writing would happen quickly, organically. I just had to trap the idea in my brain, and I'd be off!

Yeah.

It turns out that's a Big Writing Lie.

Ideas are cheap. They laze around on park benches in the sun, and they drip off the backs of toddlers in the rain. They're everywhere. Your Lyft driver will have two more for you by the time you're done reading this chapter.

Here's the truth: most of my books were each based on a ten-minute session of "OH GOD, I HAVE TO WRITE A BOOK, WHAT SHOULD IT BE ABOUT?"

***Any* idea is good enough.**

There are the blockbuster ideas: *Left behind on Mars!*

And the smaller ideas: Woman throws a dinner party on a night the power goes out.

Both of these can be equally powerful. To be honest, I'm more moved by an honest emotion felt by a woman sitting on a couch looking a dying chrysanthemum than I am by Matt Damon stranded on the red planet.

The hard part is the writing.

The hard part is getting to the computer day after day, hour after hour. The slog. (The slog ends up making magic! Never fear! But knowing that doesn't make it less difficult.)

I know it might be hard to hear, but your Big Idea isn't that special (neither is mine, neither is Gillian Flynn's). Your *writing* is what's special and unique. The idea you've been waiting to use, the one you're scared someone will steal if you tell too many people because it's *so great*? My sweet, throw it out. Think of another one. Then throw that one out, and think of another one. Do all that in the next ten minutes, then ask your barber for a character idea, and think of *another* plot idea.

Or have you been trying to fix a book you've been writing for a long time, sure that you'll never get a better idea than this one? File that book away, and *make* yourself have an idea. **Sit on the**

couch and stare at the ceiling and say "What If" fifty times. Start to add words to the end of that: *What if my mom was actually my aunt? What if a baby could fly? What if my blood started turning into stone?* Do twenty-five of these. Circle one that tickles your fancy, and start writing about it.

Knowing what idea to stick with is hard, of course. If you're writing a novel, you'll be stuck with this idea riding shotgun in your brain for a long time. The good part is this: You can change your mind at any time! Writing about ants? Decide halfway through to write about bankers? Keep writing, moving forward, as if the whole book was about bankers and then fix the first half when you hit revision.

Bottom line: Don't worry about whether your idea is good enough or not (it is). Worry about adding more words (even crappy ones—especially those!) to your manuscript.

How do you actually make yourself sit down and write? Yeah, that's the really hard part. More on that in letters to come.

Onward!

xo,

Rachael

CHAPTER SEVEN

Commitment

Hi writing friends,

"At the moment of commitment, the universe conspires to assist you." GOETHE

I often quote this phrase (it being one of the few quotes I love that's short enough to stay in my rattling brain). This quote changed my life.

There's a certain magical Universe that I don't subscribe to. I don't think that the universe is waiting to see what I pin to my mystical dream board. But, without ascribing forces to places they don't belong, even Goethe felt it.

When you commit, something commits back.

It could be as simple as observational selection bias. (You know, when you buy a new-to-you car and suddenly you see that make and model *everywhere* on the road?) Because you're more open to observation, you see what you might not have seen otherwise. I find this *all the time* in writing. I'm writing about one thing (a particular kind of frog, say), and that dang frog is *everywhere*: in songs, in billboards, on the radio, in conversations of others on the train.

So let's say this instead: **When you commit, you notice ways to keep committing.**

For me, it was sitting in an audience thinking to myself, "I'm already working as hard as I can on writing, and I just can't do more."

Then I realized: I could do more. I *had* to do more. **By saying "I can't do more" I was actually saying "I don't REALLY want to be a writer."** So I committed to getting up at an ungodly hour before work.

I kept that commitment (until I got a new job that let me sleep in a little more). Every day, even when it was the hardest thing in the world to do, I swung my feet to the floor at 3:40 in the morning. I made my bleary way to the computer. I started typing.

The very week I made that commitment, I signed with my amazing agent.

Now, I don't think the Universe handed me an agent because I deserved it for getting up earlier. After all, I'd written a book. I'd finished it. I'd revised it. I'd been submitting to agents for months.

But to me—that commitment to put my writing first (literally), choosing it over every single other thing in my life—that's what changed everything.

What are you not doing, because you think you can't?

What do you *know* the answer to this question is, even though you don't want it to be true?

It might be getting up earlier (but for your sake, I hope it isn't). It might be putting the word Writer into your LinkedIn profile. It might be telling your husband what you've been working on in secret for six months (but for the love of God, don't let him read it unless he's a writing professional and probably not even then). It might be committing (and following through) to send three query letters a week.

You know what it is—you know in your deepest heart what it's going to take to *push* you into the next step. You know what you've been failing to commit to.

So commit.

Then watch what happens when you act diligently, when you act with belief.

I'd love to hear what happens. Keep me posted.

Onward!

xo,

Rachael

CHAPTER EIGHT

Turn on the Damned Faucet

Hi writers,

I grew up in a reading household. We read everything, everywhere. On any given weekend afternoon at my house, you could find a mother and a father and three girls of varying ages reading while draped over couches and hammocks and floors.

The library couldn't hope to keep up with us. We could check out ten books each, every week, and we did, but that still wasn't enough for us. Once I'd blown through my books and my sisters', I'd raid the family room, looking for more. Anything was fair game. I read my mother's gothics (Mary Stewart and M.M. Kaye) and my dad's westerns (all Louis L'Amour, all the time).

Oh, Louis L'Amour, man of the land. He taught me so much.

He taught me that cowboys are special and that cowgirls are strong. He taught me that danger is inevitable, but so is love. He taught me that there's surprise in formula and beauty in templates.

His characters always won. That's important, you know.

"Start writing, no matter what. The water does not flow until the faucet is turned on."

This quote is his biggest gift to me. I wouldn't make it through first drafts without this quote.

Every time I face any part of a first draft, I look blankly at the page that matches my face.

Yeah, I've got nothing. Again. It's a familiar feeling.

I start typing.

Then something happens while my fingers move—thoughts come.

Big ones.

The timing isn't predictable. Sometimes my brainstorm comes ten seconds after I start typing, but more often it's about an hour or so in. *Oh!* That's why this character loves baths so much—it's because of the secret hot spring on the property which I did not know about until now but there it is. Like it's always been there (which it probably has—but I couldn't have found the spring on the property if my characters hadn't been poking around).

If my computer stays closed, I can have all manner of fleeting Grand Ideas. Some are very good, and they stick around until I get back to the page to try them out. Most aren't—they're just thoughts, wandering and mildly interesting and worth what you paid for them.

The really big thoughts? The connections that suddenly make this book fit together in great big audible *SHOOONKS*? **Those come while writing.**

It feels magical, but really, it's not.

It's entirely predictable, just as Louis L'Amour said. I guess that over the course of writing eighty-nine novels and winning the National Book Award, he figured some stuff out.

Louis L'Amour tells us to get the words flowing by opening the goddamned faucet already.

I can almost see him sitting there, perched on the edge of a trough.

He points. "Ain't you gonna even turn the handle? What do you expect's going to happen if you don't? You think you'll grow words from that there dry, parched earth? Just turn the faucet. Water's coming. Hop to it."

Hop to it, my friends.

Turn on the water already.

Catch some in a bucket that you make out of your own particular watertight imagination, and then create glorious sunsets for your bronco busters to ride off into.

Onward!

Still draped over a couch reading when not writing,

xo,

Rachael

CHAPTER NINE

We Rise

[I debated including this one. It's from a very specific moment in time, the night after the Trump election. It received, bar none, the biggest response I've ever received from an email. I sent it not only to my writer's list, but to my full mailing list including my readers. I got hundreds of unsubscribes, dozens of hateful responses, but more importantly: almost a thousand incredible responses that said *I hear you. I'm with you. I'm scared, too. Thank you.* I include it here to show that as writers, we need to lift our voices. We have a gift. We must use it. *You* must use it, even (or especially) if you believe differently than I do. If you're a Trump supporter and want to keep enjoying my work, it might be best to skip this one.]

Dear friends,

I try to keep an open mind about a great many things. I never got involved with the great green-peas-in-guacamole debate of 2014, for example. I am agnostic about jeggings. I know that people are different, with different tastes and beliefs, and the warp against the weft is what makes us interesting.

In the past, I've been able to stay that way about politics. I had a side, and I believed my side was right, naturally, but I could also *understand* the other side. On Twitter, I enjoyed sharing political cartoons lampooning the politicians I despised as much as any twitterholic. But I understood it when I saw a cartoon of Obama or Biden, an image that made them look strident or ugly or stupid. I shared the same caricatured images of Boehner and Bush. As humans, we categorize things, we make fun of things we disagree with. I believe in democracy. When Gee Dub won (even though he lost the popular vote), I was devastated, but not this way.

Then, we still had a balance of power in POTUS, Senate and House, or least a semblance of it. There were checks and balances.

Tuesday, we lost all that.

I thought of those cartoons that always look the same no matter who's being lampooned: floppy mouth, raisin eyes, angry arms. I thought to myself, *Maybe I'm overreacting.* In politics, we always think the ones we oppose are monstrous, when in reality, they're just politicians, as prone to fits of joy or slips of corruption as the rest of us. We think we're better—but we're not. We just have different beliefs, based on different teachings or books.

But this time it *is* different.

We had a few people over to watch the returns on Tuesday night. We didn't invite many. We only bought two bottles of champagne.

Yesterday I took those bottles out of the fridge, unopened, and put them in the wine rack.

I swear to God, those unopened bottles hold my heart.

Champagne triggers my migraines sometimes, and yet I couldn't wait to taste the bubbles on my lips, to know that a woman I believe in, a woman I respect so mightily, was going to be the leader of our nation.

The wrong team won.

Hillary has faults, yes. She's a politician; of course she has faults. (Could I run for that office? Could you? Hell, no. And I don't give a fuck about her emails.)

This isn't just about the wrong team winning. If a normal career politician, a regular right-wing rednecked good-old boy had won, I would be heartily disappointed. I would have cried.

But I would have been able to hold this in my mind: *We all think we're right. We're all a little wrong about that. We'll limp through. We'll be okay.*

Trump and Pence are different.

Everything has changed, and we are entering revolution.

They want to strip the rights of minorities, immigrants, the disabled, the poor, and the LGBTQ. They want to keep immigrants from seeking asylum in our country, something our country was founded upon. In a country based on systemic racism, a country just beginning a third, vastly-needed civil rights movement, they want to silence the few voices brave enough to shout against the oppression. Not only that, but with the House and Senate behind them, they will start wars against other countries and against our environment—wars we can't win. Period.

How did this happen?

Here's how: The undecideds weren't undecided. Those one in four who said they weren't sure? They were closeted. They knew enough to understand they shouldn't tell anyone they were voting for Trump. *They knew enough to be ashamed.* But in the ballot booth, alone, quietly, they voted for the white supremacist candidate.

David Duke and the KKK were elated by the win (this alone is eternally damning). Every totalitarian regime rejoiced on Wednesday. Russian leaders literally cheered when Trump won.

Hatred has been given validity.

Violence is now acceptable.

With more than half the population voting against hate, we still lost.

You have to know this: my wife and I are now scared to leave the house. We live in the Bay Area in a liberal state, and we're still terrified to hold hands in public. And we're privileged. We're white. We're still scared out of our skulls, and we ain't got nothin' on how POC are feeling (*and have been feeling*).

This week we mourn. We find community. We eat with friends. We spend our money close to home, in small businesses we care about. We pray. We meditate. We cry.

Next week?

We rise.

How? I have no freaking idea. Not yet. We're still mourning. I'm numb, the way I always get during storms of grief.

But in our house, we know this:

- Even with half the income we had last year, we're tightening belts and just set up monthly donations to Planned Parenthood and the ACLU.
- We will attend every demonstration we can. (We don't have kids—we can be arrested, but oh, the dogs would be *so pissed off* at that.)
- We will listen more than we talk.
- We will talk with those who need to be heard most.

On Wednesday, I was so upset I walked the dogs with the express intention to meet a neighbor (any neighbor, I didn't care) and talk about it. In my Oakland neighborhood, we are good at waving. We're not always so good at talking.

An older black woman I'd never spoken to was sitting on her

porch, watching her husband wash the car. I halted the dogs and stopped on the sidewalk.

"How are you?" I asked.

She waved her hand politely. "Oh, fine, fine."

"No. How *are* you? Because I'm completely devastated and I was wondering how you felt."

She looked at me in astonishment. "I'm not surprised. But it's so terrible I can't bear it."

We talked for twenty minutes. I tried to listen more than I spoke. Miss Mary E. and I are friends now. She asked what my car and house looked like because now "I can come knock if I need you."

My parents raised me on picket lines. I knew every verse to "We Shall Overcome" before I knew the names of the Disney princesses. I truly believe that my New Zealander mother, who never had the slightest interest in becoming a US citizen, would have finally become a citizen after thirty-five years of residence in order to vote against Trump.

I won't let her down.

I will do my part.

I will write.

I will march.

I will listen.

I will lift up.

What will you do?

All my love,

Rachael

PS—I know I'll get plenty of hate mail and unsubscribes from this letter. That's okay. If we disagree on this, you won't enjoy my books. (But if you hate this, please *do* feel free to leave me a book review saying that – every single review, even the bad ones, helps with visibility and sales at places like Amazon and GoodReads! Thanks!)

CHAPTER TEN

Your Superpower Is Writing

Hi writers,

You're still here! I'm so glad. I sent last week's letter to *all* my subscribers, not just to my favorites (that's you writers, each one of you), and whew! I got a lot of blowback from it. I got some angry mail, some hurt mail, and some good, old-fashioned hate mail. It was quite exciting! (Mostly, though, I got love mail. Don't worry.)

The morning after I sent it, I went to a local writer's meeting. The speaker was emphatic and tall and wore Louboutins the same way I wear wool. She spoke about growing a readership. She laid out the Dos as well as the For the Love of God Don't Dos.

"For the love of God," she said, speaking clearly and enunciating slowly. "Never ever *ever* get political with your email subscribers. Ever! That list is sacred. Don't piss them off. Get that list as big as you can, and keep it that way."

My face went red as I blushed up to my hairline. A bunch of people in that room had gotten that email. I could feel them looking at me. Sophie Littlefield, my partner in crime, nudged me cheerfully. (A good nudge is a quality skill set I require my friends to have.)

I felt guilty. Embarrassed.

Had I blown it? Had I done it wrong? (As a perpetually extroverted but shy person, I'm always way too worried about getting things right.)

As the unsubscribes and hate mail flooded in, I honestly wondered if I'd screwed up big time. Writing is my job. Readers are *so* important—they really are everything.

But I still stood by what I'd said.

I checked my gut, and it still said the same thing.

Then I saw a quote that confirmed what was in my heart:

"This is precisely the time when artists go to work. There is no time for despair, no place for self-pity, no need for silence, no room for fear. We speak, we write, we do language. That is how civilizations heal." - Toni Morrison

I'd almost forgotten my artistry while wasting time worrying about irritating people who wouldn't get an invite to my hot tub party (if I had a hot tub).

I'm a writer.

Writers write. They convince. They motivate. They speak their minds and their hearts, even when they're scared.

Like Toni Morrison said, "we do language." It's what we do.

I tripped over another quote yesterday.

"Writers, especially when they act in a body and with one direction, have great influence on the public mind." - Edmund Burke

***You* are a writer. *You* have that power.** Whether it's an email to your mother or a note to your boss, you have power. We sometimes take that power for granted—we forget that the whole world can't do this (don't doubt yourself—if you're on this list, you *can* do this).

So do a little of it.

Write a love note to your wife. Write a letter to your congressman. Write a short story. Write a poem. Write a declaration. Write a note of admiration to your neighbor who this year hung the most amazing Halloween decorations *ever*. Write in your journal.

Use your superpower. It's yours for a reason.

Onward!

xo,

Rachael

PS—Don't worry, YOU would get an invite to my hot tub party (if I had a hot tub).

CHAPTER ELEVEN

Community

Hello writing friends,

We're all about ready to scoop this year right out the door and dance on its grave, aren't we? It's been hard lately, for so many people.

There was a fire in Oakland on Friday. The death toll is thirty-six and still climbing.

When tragedy strikes, we want to help. We want to give blood even when the blood banks are full because everyone else wants to donate. We want to bring blankets to those who are cold, and we want to bring food to the workers sifting through rubble, pail by pail. My only connection to the fire is that my wife's friend's daughter died in it, and I didn't know either of them. Purely a tangential connection.

That, and we could smell the smoke when we woke.

Sometimes we have to tend to our own community. In tragedy, I always think of the dispatchers working the scene (I worked 911 for seventeen years). I knew the firefighters would be well taken care of—they always are, thank goodness. But the dispatchers are trapped in their chairs, unable to walk away and take a break, unable to stop—even just for a minute—answering the phone that never stops ringing.

So I brought treats and coffee (and a small therapy dog named Dozy) to the dispatchers who had worked a sixteen-hour night, had eight hours off (in which they commuted, ate, showered, slept, and commuted back) and were right back into their dispatch chairs. Their eyes, when I got there, were tired and sad, but really? They just looked normal. Dispatchers are used to sadness, and they're used to setting that to the side and just answering the next call, tending to the next emergency, because tragedy doesn't stop when the day is too full of it.

I don't tell you this to get applause—I'm not looking for approbation for a silly, too-easy Starbucks run. Anyone could do that.

But usually, the Someone who does the Something is part of a community.

Who is your community?

Who do you take care of?

Family? Coworkers? Great. Those are the ones you should tend to.

How about your writing community?

Do you have one?

Full disclosure: Here's where I stopped writing this draft of this letter. I thought to myself, *Hey. What if the writer reading this letter doesn't have a writing community? What should I tell her?*

Because honestly? I'm not sure I would have made it through this year without my writing friends. They are my best, deepest, and truest soul connections. They are, literally, everything to me.

I want you to have that, too.

So I'm going to encourage you to do a few things, if you don't currently have a circle of writers that loves you.

1. Join a national writing association. I personally think Romance Writers of America is the best organization around.

Even if you don't actually write romance, you can be an associate member and go to your local meetings (we have thriller, mystery, and nonfiction writers in our San Francisco group—all are welcome) to learn about the craft and the industry of writing. Also great: SFFWA, MWA, Sisters in Crime and many more. Google is your friend.

2. Go to a writing Meetup in your area. Give a business card to the person you sit down next to and say, "Oh, man, I'm so nervous. My name is ______, and here's my card. Want to chat a minute?" Almost all writers have a deep vein of introversion as well an appreciation for authenticity, and they'll respond warmly. (Don't have a business card? Go get some. Moo.com is great for cheap cards. Put your name, your email address and the word *Writer*. You're on this email list. You're a writer. I give you permission.)

3. I AM JUST SPITBALLING HERE: **What if we had a group on Facebook?**

short pause

Oh, hell, let's just have one. I took a minute to create one. I won't be *terribly* active there (because I forget for days/weeks at a time that FB exists), but I'll pop in and out. There, you can meet other writers, set your challenges and declare them, and get cheered on. Why not come over and join and introduce yourself? **Please google and then join Facebook Onward Writers!**

Come say hello to the FB group. Currently, I'm all alone over there.

Here's hoping that this year, which came in like a lion and stayed that way for most of the year, goes out like a tiny, exhausted lamb about to take a long winter's nap.

Onward!

xo,

Rachael

CHAPTER TWELVE

How to Write a Little More

Hello, writers!

Hey, *where* do you write?

Your house? The kitchen? A friend's living room? **It's not so much about having a room of one's own, it's more about knowing how to carve out a mental space within a physical one.**

Me? I have to get out of the house to create brand-new words. I can revise just about anywhere—the plane, my home office, the front seat of my car. But to capture new ideas, I have to be out of the house.

It's a little frustrating, actually. I have an amazing office. I've spent a lot of time setting it up, just so. I have a beautiful rolltop desk, and the drawers hold everything from writing gum to hair elastics. My setup is ergonomic, and my chair is comfortable.

But brand-new words don't come when I'm inside the house. Instead, the dogs distract me. The cats whine for food (silly cats, always needing "nutrition"). The dishes should probably be done, and is the washing machine really leaking? (It is.) That stack of unread writer magazines should probably be recycled or read—I might as well read a couple of them quickly.

So in order to get a first draft, I leave.

For a long time, I went to a local café. But honestly, I grew resentful about spending five dollars on a simple Americano. I'm cheap that way, and I like the coffee we drink at home. So I started pouring my coffee into my travel mug and writing at my old college, Mills, which is around the corner from where we live.

Home-brewed coffee. Big tables. And best of all, I no longer have a working Wi-Fi password for the campus.

So I go. I sit. I stare at the screen. And eventually, I get bored enough to write. There's absolutely nothing else to do. It's a trick, I know. But my brain is kind of dumb when it comes to tricks. The same trick, ten years down the road, still works.

What about you?

Is there a local library near you where you can go to work? Can you try a new café and not ask for the Wi-Fi password? Or set up a program like Freedom which removes you from the internet for whatever amount of time you set?(I love Freedom so much I've dedicated a couple of books to it, no lie.)

(No, you don't need the internet to write. Need to do research? Guess at it. Put in an asterisk, and fill in the research later.)

It always, always helps to have a plan.

Do you have one for this coming week? What if you're reading this at the holidays? The relatives are descending any minute, and you're stressed out about the shopping you still need to do, not to mention the wrapping (my family says it looks like I wrap presents with my feet, but I swear to God I'm trying as hard as I can. Scotch tape and I just don't play well together).

But do you have an extra day off work this week? Can you write on your calendar a block of time that you'll use to write, to get some words done? Even one hour is wonderful. Two stolen hours feel even better. But if you can't get that, aim for grabbing even fifteen minutes. **I've written whole books in fifteen-minute increments.** Sometimes that's just how we have to do it to get 'er done.

So block off some time. Figure out *where* you'll write.

(And then tell me how it went. I'd love to hear.)

I know you can do it.

Onward!

xo,

Rachael

CHAPTER THIRTEEN

On Screwing Up

Hi writers,

Do you ever have those self-congratulatory times when you know that you're amazing? When you know that you have this part *dialed*, and you know exactly what you're doing, you're just *so* pleased with yourself?

Yeah, me too. Five minutes later is usually when I fall flat on my face.

It's predictable, in fact.

Earlier this afternoon, I was patting myself on the back for being such a great macro creator in Microsoft Word. (A macro is a custom-built command that tells Word to do something complicated.) I can ride a macro like a rodeo rider rides a bull, and that's actually not a bad metaphor, seeing as how kludgy Word is oftentimes.

"I shouldn't think this," I thought. "There's going to be a major problem."

Uh-huh. After spending several hours formatting a new book for both print and epub, I was done. I uploaded the files to

Amazon, Kobo, iBooks, Nook, and Google Play. Woot! I was a *whiz*. I was *smug*.

Then I noticed that something in my macro had removed the last piece of punctuation from every single chapter.

Oh, and I had deleted all italics in the entire document.

You know me and italics. I *love* italics. Basically, *I live my life italicized.*

I'm not the kind of person to throw chairs against the wall. Anger comes very slowly to me, and I don't get mad at dumb mistakes like that one.

I do get frustrated, though. Just when I feel like I have something down, I don't.

Just when I feel like I know how to write a book, I start writing a book that's agony from start to finish, and there's no rhyme or reason to it. The last two books have been pretty easy, and I'm worried about what might be coming.

But you know what? I'm not afraid to screw it all up.

What's the worst that could happen? (Oh, god, no, *don't* actually think about what the worst is. You're a writer. Your imagination is good. Don't go there.) But trust me, failing at writing things is way easier to fix than say, failing at marriage, or friendship, or trust.

Life doesn't have a backspace key. Writing does.

Just trust me when I say you're going to fail. We all are, over and over again. And it's okay.

Remember when you were a kid and you thought it would be a good idea to try to roller-skate down that big hill? Yeah. You got bloodied up. Maybe a black eye. And then you went out the next day and maybe you had a little more respect for the hill. When you tried it on your bike, you rode your brakes hard the first time, but then you got to the point where you could sail down that hill like a plane coming in to land.

Getting something down cold doesn't mean you won't crash and burn again.

It just means that you're less scared to get banged up.

We're tough. We're made that way. You've lived this long in this rough world? Dude, you have *so* much stamina and so much to say.

Do the work, no matter how worried you are that you're going to get it all wrong. (Because you will, and that's wonderful, and that will show you something new.)

Don't let Resistance take you down (have you read Steven Pressfield's book, *The War of Art*? You should). As my friend Aaron H. said after reading it, "It's weird how I can motivate myself to get up every morning and show up at a place to work in a job I really don't care for, but can't motivate myself to do something I've wanted to do since I was twelve years old!"

Resistance is hard. But remember, every single one of us feels the same way you do.

Show up.

Do the work.

Screw it up and groan and make another cup of tea and fix it tomorrow.

You can do this.

And don't forget to check that you didn't leave out the punctuation. ;)

Onward!

xo,

Rachael

CHAPTER FOURTEEN

Wrangling Time Like the Varmint It Is

Hi writers,

I started tracking my time in earnest this month, and it's had a huge effect on my life almost instantly. It's like when I started using the app You Need a Budget–I'd never really *understood* money and debt until I started tracking it. Toggl for time tracking is doing the same thing to my brain, and I'm really *thinking* about the way I use my hours.

Biggest surprise so far?

A lot of time blocks I didn't consider work actually *are* part of my work. Earlier this week, I had to send an international wire transfer to reserve a block of rooms for a Venice writing retreat. I found that my credit union had stopped doing them, and I had to literally switch banks in order to get it done. That was three hours that I would normally have just whined about, three hours lost from my work time.

That banking kerfuffle? That *was* work time.

Mind = blown.

Did you read the article, *"Why Time Management is Ruining our Lives"*? (*The Guardian*, December 2016)

Oy. To know that even productivity guru Merlin Mann wishes he hadn't gone quite so far down the productivity wormhole? That was rough to read.

I worship time management. I bow at its altar and offer my pittance of minutes stolen from the recesses of my Midori Bullet Journal. Even as a kid, I was obsessed with getting the most from time, wringing every possible drop from the hours I was allotted. I loved *Cheaper by the Dozen* and its look at Frank Bunker Gilbreth Sr.'s early study of time and motion. I walked around the house making sure to batch my trips. Going downstairs to get a snack? I'd carry two books that had to go to the living room and bring back upstairs both my snack and my laundry. (This was when I was about nine, mind you.)

So I listened with bated breath this week as Kim Werker told me about her foray into time management with the app Asana. Maybe this would be it! Maybe this would be the one thing that finally got my time whipped into shape.

Because I've been needing *help*.

I've always been good at managing my time. I'm not the kind of person who looks down at a pencil and looks up to find the sun is setting outside.

But I've been scheduling too much.

I've forgotten what I can and can't do. I'm used to over-reaching and *just* getting what I want *right* before I fall out of the tree, and I have to say, that method is exhausting and leaves bruises.

Every year, I choose a word that I'll keep in mind for the next year. A few years ago, the word was *BRAVE* because I knew I'd have to be courageous to leave my day job.

This year doesn't seem to have a word for me. Instead, it has a phrase:

"Can I do less?"

This is totally contrary to what I've ever done.

But it feels right.

I'll still do everything, don't get me wrong. I have plans to write three (maybe four) books this year, and I'm releasing three. I have two podcasts. I'm teaching at Stanford and Berkeley. I write an essay a month for Patreon. I'm creating a new online class.

How am I supposed to do all this and *still* do less within a day?

While talking to Kim, she said her assistant had built her schedule for her, including buffer room.

Wiggle room!

I never give myself *any* of that. My days are constantly scheduled full, from top to bottom. I work right up to every deadline I've ever had. When I get a migraine and lose two days, my whole schedule is hosed, and I have to redo everything.

This year, no.

This year, I'm building wiggle room into:

- my deadlines (two weeks of it)
- my weeks (one day a week, unscheduled, to be filled as needed)
- my days (TWO OPEN HOURS planned, every work day. That can be used to do the things I didn't see coming—and there are always tons of those every week, or to read—part of the job!— or to nap—part of a good life!)

I'm scheduling three hours of *Deep Work* (an excellent book by Cal Newport) into each morning. That time is strictly to do writing of new words and revision of old ones. The rest of my work hours are scheduled for tasks, the myriad things that keep my world turning 'round and money flowing in.

Thanks to a suggestion from my mastermind group, I'm going to try to keep one day a week completely unscheduled (besides the deep work time). As it stands right now, that may be a different day each week, but that day can catch some of the flotsam and jetsam of the rest of the week.

I'm going to use a combination of Asana (for the reminders it sends) and my Bullet Journal to track my time. [Update–I switched from Asana to OmniFocus for a sturdier project management system but still love Toggl for the time tracking.]

I'm going to give myself more time.

I'm going to schedule downtime, every day.

I'll keep you posted as to how it goes. How about you? How do you plan out your time? I'd love to hear.

xo,

Rachael

PS–I realize that I'm whining about time management when writing is my full-time job. I understand the place of privilege I'm in, and *boy*, do I appreciate it and never take it for granted.

PPS–I have a *new* writing podcast in addition to *How Do You Write*, did you know that? J. Thorn and I are talking about making the transition to writing full time over at *The Petal to the Metal*. Come listen. We're funny together.

CHAPTER FIFTEEN

Your Writing Routine

Hi writers,

I got an email earlier this week from someone trying to sell me something that asked me what my writing routine was. The goal of that email was to get me to buy a piece of software that would improve my writing routine. (Before you ask, you don't need the software, I promise, or I would totally tell you about it.)

But it got me thinking about rituals.

A ritual is a ceremony that is made of actions performed in a prescribed manner.

And oh, lordy, do I love a ritual.

I have so many in my life. A sampling:

- The way I push the dogs out of my office every morning to lay out my yoga mat and move my body around for thirty minutes.
- The way I heat my oatmeal for four minutes exactly, and *then* add the frozen blueberries so I get an infusion

of insta-cool which means I can get to the eating part of my day faster.
- The way I polish my glasses when thinking about emotion, as if that would make it easier for me to see.

I like rituals with everything, everywhere.

When I'm in a strange city, I set up a routine on the very first day. I unpack my clothes, putting them into drawers and setting my paperwork in order on whatever desk I have nearby. I find a new "favorite" cafe and go back often. I used to bring a scented candle when I traveled until I almost started my agent's apartment on fire (true story) and now I don't bring extra flames with me. I even unpack in a tent.

And I really love my writing routine, *which is always changing.*

I know that's contrary to the usual advice of "always play the same music" or "always have the same scent in the air." Shouldn't writing rituals be rules that you've set yourself and that you follow, hard and fast?

Look. **Life isn't static.** It's always, always changing. If I'd made myself stick to the same cafe where I used to get excellent work done, I'd be there right now, hating the smell of onions (they added cooked food to the menu) and distracted by the woman talking to herself while wearing intricately crafted items made from foil (bless her, but I can't tune her out even with white noise turned up to eleven).

If I'd made myself stick to writing at four in the morning., I'd BE VERY SAD AND TIRED.

If I'd made myself stick to writing when the mood struck, I'd have no books written at all.

Old rituals die. New ones rise to take their place. That's natural.

I've recently learned that the best routine for me in writing is putting my feet up. Who knew? It seems, for me, that sitting with feet down means email and tasks. Feet up (or standing) means making new words. (You can't really do the feet-up thing if you're in a cafe or you turn into one of *those* people, like the people who Skype without headphones in public.)

My routine, though solid and predictable on a daily basis, changes over the long term. It's always moving, always a work in progress.

That's okay. That's *good*. That's life.

I will admit that a few things always remain, though, and I'll list them here in case they're of use to you:

- I use Write or Die to catch my first drafts. No jump-scares, no kamikaze mode, I just have the screen go to red when I'm not writing, and I get a puppy image when I'm done.
- I use Post-its like some people put parmesan on pasta —everywhere, with gusto.
- I write in silence at home, and with white noise when I'm out. (I used to write more often with music, but lately I can hear the rhythm of my words better with no melody at all.)
- I use Sharpwriter pencils. Always Sharpwriter. Plain, cheap, basic, reliable. (Like me!)
- Scent *is* helpful for me, so I burn incense or put a pan of cinnamon/clove water on a low burner (CAUTION: FLAMES!). It's not so much what it smells like as the fact that the air just smells nice.

Don't worry if you're still finding your way into your perfect writing routine. If it's changing, that's good.

Play.

Explore.

Experiment.

Onward!

xo,

Rachael

CHAPTER SIXTEEN

You Can't Help Getting Better at Writing

Hi writers,

If you write, you can't help getting better at writing.

It's true.

I was talking to some folks from the NaNoWriMo office yesterday at a lunchtime meeting, and we were talking about this very thing.

The more you write, the better you get.

It doesn't really make intuitive sense, and it's one-hundred percent fine if you don't believe it. That's the nice thing. It works even if you think it's a bunch of hooting malarky.

It just happens. I think of it like when we learned to walk. (I take a lot of metaphors back to when we were children, because it works. Writing is a lot like child's play, only, you know, WAY HARDER. But we do it because we're drawn to it, the same reason we splashed in puddles and cut the cat's whiskers.)

When we learned to walk, we wobbled for a long time. We took those wide, waddling steps and thumped backward onto our butts regularly and often.

You know what we didn't do?

We didn't sit around and think about it. *I wonder exactly in which direction I should point my toes for maximum acceleration? How would it go it I pulled myself up with my right hand, and not with my left? Why is this cat food here? Should I eat it, or will it make my stomach feel upset later?*

No. We just walked. We ate the cat food. We walked some more, and by doing it, we just got better at it.

Eventually, we could run. Skip. Hop. We learned how to balance on the edges of sidewalks and not step on the cracks because we didn't want to break our mother's backs, and we learned how to leap from stone to slippery stone in the creek. We weren't taking classes, and we weren't reading *The Art and Craft of Human Mobility*. We weren't listening to podcasts about it or going to meetings to learn about the craft of walking.

We just walked a lot. And we got better at it.

It's exactly the same with writing.

A number of years ago, I wanted to make some money. I wanted to get into the self-publishing business. I had romance writing friends who were cleaning up, and I wanted to see if I could make some money, too.

I wanted to write a lot of books, fast. Back then, the magic formula (pro tip = there *is* no magic formula) was to release five books at once for maximum sales algorithm velocity.

So I wrote four books and a novella. I wrote them as fast as I could, at lightning speed. No book took more than six weeks, and a couple of them were done and dusted within a month.

I took a pen name, because I didn't want this fast writing to "cheapen" my real name. I assumed because I wrote them so quickly, they'd be below the Rachael Herron standard I tried to maintain, whatever the hell that meant to me then.

You know what?

Those books were good.

They were as strong as anything else I'd ever written (and in some ways, they were better). Eventually, due to many Publishing Reasons too boring to go into, I brought them over to my real name and killed the pen name.

Just writing those books made me a better writer.

I know this because I put no extra learning into the craft, bringing nothing with me except what I already knew. I didn't take classes on plotting or character arc. *whispers* I didn't even *try* to make them incredibly good. I just wrote, in the voice I naturally write in.

But by simply writing, I learned, automatically.

That's all it took.

How do you become a better writer? You write. If you're writing, guaranteed, you're getting better.

Isn't that awesome? Don't you feel a little let off the hook for figuring out how to make your writing stronger? Just write!

So get to writing, my friends.

Onward!

xo,

Rachael

CHAPTER SEVENTEEN

Read Like It's Your Job

Dear writers,

Sometimes I'm so busy being focused on writing that I forget reading is actually part of my job.

Reading's part of *your* job, too.

There's a school of thought in Creative Writing Land that says what you read will be what you produce. A kind of garbage-in-garbage-out rule.

I don't believe that, though I *do* think our tastes change the better we get at this writing gig.

Here's the thing. The more you write, the better you get at writing. The better you get at writing, the better you get at *reading*. **At some point, you *will* find that books aren't making you happy on levels that didn't bother you in the past.** That author you loved so much? Maybe you've learned all you can from him. That's okay. The series you couldn't get enough of last year? Maybe you've noticed that the characters are just a little bit flat. If you were writing them, you'd do it differently.

You'd make her sing instead of whine. You'd make him more silly and less serious.

It's a problem.

One of my favorite professors in college was Al Landwehr. Now my friend, he taught me how to *really* read. He taught me that when a passage moved me, I should go back to it and tug at all its parts. I should treat it like a puzzle box, figuring out exactly how which part fit into which other bit.

He'd sit back in his chair and laugh at us. We had those small chair-desks, the kind with the perennial bubblegum that would get stuck to your knee if you crossed your legs. He'd put us in a circle, and he'd sit in one of those desks, too. We'd talk about Andre Dubus and Margaret Atwood and Alice Munro, and he'd watch us get excited, get confused, and most of all, get inspired.

"I've ruined you!" he'd trumpet excitedly. "You'll never enjoy just reading for the hell of it again!"

And he was, in many ways, right.

Not that reading closely as a writer ruined my enjoyment. Of course not—it made it that much more enjoyable. But it's true, I don't very often lose myself in plot anymore.

I do, though, still lose myself in language, and isn't that one of the most sublime pleasures available to us as humans? (You're reading this letter—I know you already know this about language and the way it moves us.)

You may have been noticing it as you write more.

Books are harder to get into.

They're more difficult to stick with.

You have a *lot* less patience with clichés and characters who sulk and complain without a very good reason.

You throw more books against the wall (I've only ever done this with one book in my life, and it was *Lonesome Dove*, and it was because Larry McMurtry broke my damn heart and I've never been angrier at a writer in my life but in that instance it was because he wrote so well, not so poorly).

You have to look harder for books that enchant you, that you want to sink into, that you don't want to pull apart with your teeth to see how the insides work.

That's the bad news.

The good news?

There are *so* many writers out there you just have to poke around to find what you're looking for.

Don't waste time finishing books you're not loving (some make an argument that you can learn how *not* to write that way, but life is short, yo. Read happy).

Read what makes your heart sing.

Read what terrifies you.

Read what makes you think.

And get some more reading done this weekend, if you can. Sink deep into the couch and make sure there's a pet of some sort on your chest, and read till your eyeballs are dry. That's my plan, for sure, on this dark, rainy weekend.

Onward!

xo,

Rachael

CHAPTER EIGHTEEN

This Is What We Get Wrong About Writing

Hi writers,

I just finished writing a Patreon essay. You may have heard me talking about them on my podcast. I love writing them *so* much though they're not easy to write (is anything?).

In this latest Patreon essay, I write about how bad we are, as humans, at predicting what will actually make us happy. I won't go into the science of it here, but this is the main takeaway: **We guess wildly at what will make us happy, and then we get it wrong, over and over again.** It's human nature, and it's part of the way we work.

It might sound familiar to you.

We dream of the totally free Saturday afternoon when the spouse has the kids, and we have the cafe. You know exactly how it will go. You'll get there, grab your favorite chair by the outlet, and you'll proceed to write the brilliant prose you know you're capable of. It will be everything you've been waiting for.

But it doesn't go like that, does it? Even when the seat is open, and your computer is plugged in, and your latte is perfect, something isn't quite right. It's your brain. It won't settle. It won't do what you *need* it to do, which is to get some goddamn words on the page that don't suck all the suckitude of suckery sucktown.

We predict what will make us happy (or sad) and we are wrong, over and over again.

It helps me to know this.

Nothing is going to go the exact way I imagine it will, either for the good or the bad, and that kind of lets me off the worry hook.

Brain science shows us that the thing you fear the most won't be as bad as you think it will be. It also shows us that the fantasy —the lottery win, the subsequent small-island purchase—*also* won't be as good as we think it will.

That means all you have is now. This imperfect, perfect moment you're sitting in right now.

Now is all.

Don't wait for after retirement. Or next weekend. Or when the kids are in grade school. Whatever you're waiting for, it's not enough.

If you're waiting for a future time, when you'll be a better writer with more discipline and courage and creativity?

The only way you're going to be one is to write messily, sloppily, and badly NOW.

Go write something. Anything. A blog post. A letter to your aunt who would die of shock if she got something in the mail from you. A love letter. A letter to the editor. A Facebook post that *says* something instead of just a status update. The first chapter of your book (it will be terrible! It's supposed to be, I promise!).

You have right now. And it's better than okay—it's all you need.

Onward!

xo,

Rachael

PS – Curious about the longform essay on this which includes things like the way I use my ADHD for my writing benefit? You can read it and all the back issues (or listen to the MP3) at Patreon.com/Rachael for as little as a buck.

CHAPTER NINETEEN

Do the Edges First

Hi writers,

I'm upstairs on the second floor of the library, looking down into the sunshine that's back in place in Northern California. It's bright out, and people are wearing their short sleeves for the first time in months. I can see three people napping in the sun, and tonight people will look in the mirror to see their first spring sunburn (I might be one of them, having forgotten sunscreen).

It's cheery. Happy.

Which is good because I just had a *hell* of a terrible time writing.

Today was just miserable.

I'm just past fifty-thousand words of this novel, a little more than halfway through, and this is always the point at which I start to doubt every single thing I've done so far.

My brain says:

- This is a terrible book.
- No one cares about this topic.

- No one will like these characters.
- I'm a terrible writer.
- How on earth am I going to make all these moving parts fit together?
- How will I fix this huge mess I'm making?

Then I remembered something I heard Ann Hood say: she likened her writing to a jigsaw puzzle, and it really affected me.

Think about your last jigsaw: there are so many pieces, all in disarray. It looks like a hot mess when dumped out on the table, all the cardboard sides showing, sticking together in clumps formed while the box was in transit.

"Just do the edges first," Ann Hood said.

It felt so good to hear—so right.

We have an idea when we start. We know what the book (or story, or poem, or article) will be like because we can see the box in our mind's eye. Oh, it's a *glorious* story! Just wait till we get it on the page! Readers will revel in the ups, and they'll weep at the downs. Our mailboxes, both physical and virtual, will overflow with fan letters, and readers will recognize us on the street.

Then we sit down to work on the book, and instead, we have all these damn pieces that don't seem like they even came from the same puzzle box we bought.

So we do the edges.

There. We have a frame.

We start to fill in the easy parts. The yellow bit of the house. The blue of that bird's wing. It's coming together.

And then? Every single time, a cat comes along when I'm about halfway done and decides to knock all of it to the floor.

It's a total mess, all over again.

What's more, I'm pretty convinced that this puzzle isn't worth it. I've worked *so* hard on it, and it took all my brain cells, and it *still* sucks, so I might as well just shove the pieces back into the box and put it in the time-out zone where it will live for the next ten years.

It's tempting. It's *so* tempting to give up and start a different puzzle. One that's easier, one that's more like the other puzzles I've done.

But I'm a stubborn jackass, so I pick up all the pieces, and I start on that damn edge again.

And in my book, I do the same thing. I go back to pen and paper. I look at my theme and hold it to the light. I inspect my characters for new flaws, ones I didn't see coming. I rejigger my plot so that it hangs better on the pegs I've hung it from.

I just keep working.

Like a puzzle, it's engrossing. I lose time as I'm moving parts around. Five minutes later, I look up to find an hour has passed.

Here's my point: Yeah, it's a mess. Yeah, it doesn't look good. Yeah, your neck gets all kinked up and your back hurts and you wonder what the hell you're doing wasting this time that you could be out learning how to play tennis or how to paint.

But when the pieces start clicking together?

That makes it all worth it.

(I'm using this as a reminder to myself, because today's writing was agony, and nothing clicked. Okay, not true: one teeny *tiny* thing clicked, and that thing made the session worthwhile. Mostly.)

Sometimes it sucks.

So just work on the edge pieces.

Onward!

xo,

Rachael

CHAPTER TWENTY

Mitten in Tree

Hi dear readers,

California has been soggy this year.

We don't know how to handle this. I've been on the freeway when the rain starts, and traffic instantly slows to a crawl. Snails zoom by, honking their horns and shaking their little slimy fists. I'm always tricked and I think there must be an accident ahead, but there seldom is. It's just us fool Californians, terrified by water **gasp** under our tires.

When I was at Mills a month or so ago (I love to write in the library there—I never spent any time in it at all when I was in grad school, but I'm making up for that now), I spotted a tiny mitten lying in a puddle. It was dark blue, and even though it was shriveled and dark in the water, I could tell it was hand knit.

So I stopped and picked it up (which I would *not* have done with a machine-knit mitten, boy howdy) and hung it at eye level in a burl of the nearest tree.

I didn't think much more about it.

Two weeks later, the rain had stopped, briefly, but it was still cold. I walked toward the library, all bundled up in a heavy sweater and cashmere scarf.

Coming toward me was a family: Mom, Dad, a baby in a stroller, and an elderly woman who looked like grandma. I like to watch people (naturally, as all writers do), so I kept my eyes on them as they approached.

The mother stopped dead. She stared at a tree.

She reached up.

She pulled out the mitten.

In a British accent, she exclaimed, "Look, darling! It's your mitten!"

Dad said, "No, it couldn't be!"

Grandma said, "Oh, my goodness!"

Baby said, "Grcckkk!"

I said as I passed the group, "I put that there."

Because I was also thinking about my book, I just kept walking for a moment, guessing that was all I should contribute to the conversation but Mom said, "Wait, *what?*"

I turned. "Oh! Yeah, I picked that up in a puddle a few weeks back." I tugged on my cabled sweater and plucked at my blue scarf. "I'm a big knitter. I knew it was precious."

Mom stared.

Grandma said, "I already made another one, but now we have a spare!" Delight was in every word (she was British too, for extra adorableness).

"Of course you did! That's what I would have done." I turned to go again.

The mother finally said, "Don't you think this is *odd*? That you found it and saved it, and then you saw us find it?"

Here's the thing: It didn't really strike me as odd.

It struck me as just lovely luck.

I'd done a (very, *very*) small thing, and by luck, I'd gotten to see the end result. It was a happy coincidence. Nothing more.

But boy, was it gorgeous. And wow, were the smiles they gave me lovely. We waved goodbye. Laughter filtered through the air between us, and I went into the library feeling warmed and happy.

It was a *connection*. One I hadn't hoped to make—how could I have predicted that?

I think about this with my books, too.

They're connections I make with *you*.

I can't plan them, and I can't coordinate them. I can't predict that *you* are the person who will pick up my book in a used bookstore and read it and like it. I can't tell you which people have their noses in one of my plots at this very moment. I can't predict if you'll like one of my novels, let alone love it. I can't see into your life to know what's going on in the background while you're reading something I wrote.

But that doesn't stop us from having that connection, and it's one of the brightest spots in my career. Me writing. You reading.

The occasional chance for us to meet in passing, to exclaim with wonder, to have that laughter strung between us, like strands of twinkling white lights, is literally why I keep writing.

So for you today, I wish a day of synchronicity, of interesting and surprising connections made when you least expect it. And lots of laughter.

Onward!

xo,

Rachael

CHAPTER TWENTY-ONE

This Is What Makes You Worthy of Being a Writer

I had a bad virus this past week. Okay, I say bad, but it wasn't the stomach flu, and it didn't come with a high, terrible fever.

It just enervated me, leaving me spent and mostly useless. I lay around like a Victorian damsel on a fainting couch. I groaned intermittently, pleased with the hoarseness of my voice. I sighed a *lot* and blew my nose like the trumpets at the gates of Zion.

Then, when I started to feel better, I stayed down. (Okay, this is a lie. Friday night, I went to see Kate Tempest at a club and *passed out.* I hadn't even had a drink. Just. Passed. Out. I have to tell you, fainting is not as cool as it's cracked up to be. In a moment that is funny in retrospect, I knew it was coming and apparently told my wife I thought I was going to faint—I barely remember this—so she had time to tell a stranger "Here, hold my drink," as she caught me, which is why she still had her Manhattan after they carted me outside for air.)

So for the weekend, I kept resting.

Even though I felt guilty about it.

You see, I measure my life by the Things I Do.

You might feel me on this one.

On Saturday, while resting, I made great cheese (coconut cheese that is healthy and tastes like the best/worst kind of nacho cheese ever—it is AMAZING) and terrible muffins, and besides that, I stayed in bed and watched *The Americans* on my phone.

It was okay that I stayed in bed because I could look to an accomplishment. I had cooked. I had baked. That made me worthwhile, as a person.

On Sunday, I was almost better. I could have powered through almost anything, given the right dose of DayQuil and liberal distribution of hoarse groans.

But instead, I didn't.

I just stayed down. I watched TV on my phone. I read. I napped a bit. I groused pleasantly and petted the animals that piled happily on top of me.

I got NOTHING done. Not one single thing.

I was feeling awful about this until I saw a tweet in my timeline. Bethany D. Lipka said, **"If all you do today is take care of yourself, your day has been productive."**

This blew my mind.

Did she mean that lying in bed was actually a Thing To Do? A thing I could be proud of?

Yes, she certainly did.

So it got me thinking.

Everyone is inherently worthy, with or without being productive.

This is something I've always believed.

Except about myself.

For me to be worthy, I have to make. (Many creative people feel this way. You might.) I have to sew a dress or bake bread or write a book or make a podcast.

Otherwise, how will my worth be tangible? How will I prove it?

This is what I realized this weekend: I need to work on loosening my grasp on this belief.

I am worthy when I write books.

I am also *equally* worthy when I do absolutely nothing.

We could dive into the field-lying-fallow metaphor, but that one has always rung hollow to me. Yo, have you met me? I AM NEVER GOING TO LET A FIELD LIE FALLOW. I will add fertilizer (organic!) to that shit (get it?) and get back in there as soon as possible.

So let's use the sleep metaphor. Our brains and bodies need sleep. We *have* to rest. And sometimes, we need more rest than we're used to giving ourselves.

I'm my own boss, have been for the last two-plus years.

And I'm also my only full-time employee.

I've got to take care of both the boss and the employee residing in this body. Sometimes I need a vacation even without going out of town. Sometimes I need an extra hour of sleep or a whole weekend in bed.

Sometimes accomplishing *nothing* is the absolute best thing for me To Do.

I am worthy, no matter what I make or don't make. No matter what I do or don't accomplish. No matter what I write or don't write.

So are you.

If you're beating yourself up, stop it. You're already worthy of being a writer. You ARE a writer. Write a little bit.

Rest, if you need it.

Then rest some more.

(Of course, ask yourself honestly if you're resting or procrastinating. You'll know the answer, deep in your heart. And depression is a different beast entirely. Good lord, if you're fighting depression and taking care of yourself by resting? GOOD FOR YOU. Don't have a *second* of regret about that.)

If all you do today is take care of yourself, you're being productive.

I believe this. And I'm going to try to remember it, too.

Take care of yourselves, dear ones.

Onward!

xo,

Rachael

CHAPTER TWENTY-TWO

I Know You Don't Want to Write

Hello, writers!

I'm back from my writing retreat in Venice, which went *spectacularly.* The people who came were amazing, and together, we inspired the lids off each other. The tops of our souls were opened up, we looked inside each other, and we came away better for the seeing and hearing and writing we'd done. We'd write all morning and get lost in the Venice *calli* all afternoon and evening. The weather was perfect. Our pens were fresh and new. Our pages turned from blank to scribbled-upon. The water rose and fell and rose again, as our hearts did the same.

It was my first time leading a retreat.

I've done a lot of teaching, so I had that to rely on, but this was my first time being The Organizer (let's not talk about the $11,000 wire transfer that was *lost* for three weeks before it was found, holy helen in a handbasin. My hair is whiter now).

And I loved every single minute of it.

Since then, though, I've done another writing retreat. Okay, the second one was just for one person, but she can be kind of a whiner, so I'm glad she enjoyed it. That retreat—of course—was for me. Seven days in Venice, mostly by myself, to rest, to write, and to wander. I wanted to fill the well. And boy, howdy, did I.

I got two book ideas out of it, and I filled a whole notebook. I wandered when and where I felt like it. I took notes on everything from the noise inside of my cluttered mind to the sound of the seagulls arguing over the fish market.

And every night, I'd look out the windows of my wee apartment onto the Grand Canal and think, "How did this happen to me?"

Luck, luck, nothing but luck, one voice answered me.

Hard work, another one said.

The truth is somewhere in the middle.

I've worked my ass off. And I've gotten really lucky in many, many ways.

But the one thing I know that's been one of the biggest helps to me is this: **You never feel like doing your heart's work.** (Okay, sometimes you do, but those times are *very* rare and can be relied on exactly as much as you rely on your Uncle Earl to not spit off the porch.)

I just watched a great TED talk on this (How to Stop Screwing Yourself Over, Mel Robbins), and she says exactly what I've felt so many times:

We get in ruts because they're comfortable. Auto-pilot is our default setting and it feels good. Doing something new/different is really hard.

And if you wait to feel like writing?

You won't write.

You just won't.

No one feels like writing. It's hard almost every single time we sit down to do it. This very letter, in fact, I started this morning and gave up ten minutes into it. I walked the dogs, I recorded a podcast, and I took a nap before I made myself get back here to finish it.

You will *not* get what you want unless you *make* yourself move toward it.

The funny thing is, this applies to almost everything that's outside our routine.

There was *nothing* I wanted more in the whole world than to lead a writing retreat in Venice. I would say it's up there with those bucket-list items you don't really think will ever happen to you, like sleeping in one of those clear-ceilinged hotels under the Northern Lights.

But I didn't want to get on the plane to go. (When I was on the plane, however, I was nothing but excited.) I was overwhelmed thinking about how much work it would be. (When I was working, it was energizing, not exhausting.)

That first night, when I set out the prosecco and strawberries at our get-to-know-you meeting, I had to keep my knees locked to keep from running away. (When we were all chatting, of course, it was exciting and fun.)

I did *not* want to walk into our meeting room that first morning. (When we were writing together, of course, it was wonderful.)

I couldn't wait until I *felt* like doing any of these things. I had to make myself. And the rewards were above anything I could have imagined.

I can't wait until I feel like writing a book to write one. I have to make myself work, daily. As the speaker says in TED talk linked above, we have five seconds to make that choice. **Feel the impulse, *move toward it* within five seconds, or you're going to slip back into your status quo.**

Watch the video linked above, and see if it sparks anything for you.

When you're done, you can watch my video-podcast of the latest How Do You Write episode, which I shot from the Venice apartment, in which I was still giddy even though I was in my last hour of being in my favorite city. (rachaelherron.com/ep043)

This Monday morning? Maybe don't hit snooze on your alarm clock, or your life. *Make yourself.* See what happens.

Love and prosecco,

xo,

Rachael

CHAPTER TWENTY-THREE

Learn How to Edit AND Pack For Your Next Trip!

Hi writers,

Oof, I had a doozy of a week, but it's looking up now. I'm over my jet lag and getting over some other physical (and mental) stumbling blocks, and I'm *back* in the driver's seat of this rattly old jalopy made of words and ink and brain cells.

My agent and I are working on a proposal, and we're making sure these are the best pages I can produce. Susanna is usually quite happy to let me get away with stuff, knowing my editor will rein me in, but this time she had to do the job, and she tore my pages *up*.

Everything my agent said to get rid of, I loved. All my beautifully-turned phrases, all my gorgeous repetitions, all the backstory on Gloria *who is an amazing character* but really, not very important, she said to get rid of them. She wanted me to tighten the hospital scene. Cut the dross (the lovely, lovely dross). Get in, get out, get back to the action.

For me, as a *feelings* kind of writer, this was both difficult and exhilarating. It was hard because I've revised these seventy-five pages a few times now (not something I normally do while writing a first draft) and I'm now fond of how the words lie on the page (one of the dangers of revision!). I've draped them so artistically and I like where they are, how they sparkle in the sun.

But it was exhilarating because I got to clear house. *Whap! Slash! Rip! Tear!* Those words/phrases/sentences/paragraphs/pages are OUT!

Which got me thinking.

The reason I love thinking about travel packing (and you *know* I am not kidding when I say I do) is because **it's about culling.**

Love that dress? Sure! Put it in the suitcase! But it is *not* coming if it can't be worn three different ways. It must also be wrinkle-resistant and easy to wash in a bathroom sink. Also, it has to be really cute (natch). Seventy-thousand bonus points for capacious pockets.

That doesn't *stop* me from putting the black-and-white striped jumper dress in the suitcase. Indeed, I put it there with relish! I can't *wait* to wear this dress on my trip!

Then I give it some time. I think about it.

It's a heavy dress. It will be obvious, because of its bold stripes, that it's the same dress no matter how I style it. It would be difficult to wash and dry overnight.

So eventually, with great muttering, I take it out of the suitcase.

It's not to say I don't love the dress—I do. It looks amazing with my black and white Fluevogs flats and it's whimsical but not silly. And it's not like I won't wear it in the future! I will! Maybe I'll wear it tomorrow! (That would show everyone!)

But it doesn't belong in this suitcase now.

It's not personal.

I'm just culling down to the bare minimum. Everything that goes in that suitcase has to have an essential job, and even better if it serves more than one.

Just like in writing.

My character Gloria was well crafted as a rape-crisis advocate. I'd want her as a friend. She broke the mold a little. But her story didn't do enough for *my* story to warrant keeping her in all her Gloria-ness, so now she's just a very minor player again, as she should have been at first.

Then I looked at every sentence in the hospital scene, holding each up to the light to look for holes, to look for *any* kind of reason at all not to place it back in the manuscript. If it wasn't perfect, if it didn't please me completely, it didn't stay.

And the work is so much better for it now.

Sometimes we all get lazy. We bring the big suitcase on the trip, or even worse, we don't make any decisions at all, and bring two or three suitcases (the horror!).

Or we write good sentences and let them all stay without them earning their space on the page. **Lazy is okay when packing or drafting, but before you or your book takes a trip, YOU MUST EDIT.**

Uh-oh, are you now worried you're not clearing out enough dead wood when you're first-drafting? Don't. This letter isn't intended to make you feel that way. Put it *all* in, put it all on the page, don't worry about a thing until you're in editing mode, which I think is best done when the book is complete, *unless* you edit as you go *and* you're getting books done (the "and" has to be there), then that's your excellent process and stick to it.

Later, you'll come back, after you've filled the suitcase full of words, and you'll have a clear-eyed look. Will I actually use two shawls, or will I wear the red one constantly like I always do? Do I need that vignette about Mr. Bodkin and the village cat, or was it just something fun to write that doesn't actually serve my plot arc very well even though the prose is lovely?

If you're drafting, these are questions for another day. For now, just fill the suitcase and the floor around it.

Later, edit mercilessly. Go all Marie Kondo with your sentences in revision (sadly, I am not even kidding with this). But instead of keeping sentences that bring you joy (because that could be *all* of them in some frames of mind), **keep the sentences that are the hardest workers.**

Keep the words that do triple duty and are wrinkle resistant and dry easily overnight.

Write a sparkly, overly-full first draft, the kind that gets stuck on the airport escalators, and later, edit it to a lean pilot's bag that acts like a TARDIS but can be swung over your shoulder if you're running through the airport late for a flight.

(Sparkles, by the way, fit in any bag. Or book, for that matter.)

Onward!

xo,

Rachael

CHAPTER TWENTY-FOUR

Once, I Literally Kicked My Book's Ass

Hi writers,

I spent thirty hours over the last few days assisting a self-defense course. At IMPACT Bay Area, they teach women to hit things (okay, people) full-force, setting boundaries and defending them, with just the weapons they're born equipped with: their hands, legs, and most importantly, their *voices.*

It's amazing. I've written about it before, several times, and if you want to see me kick some ass, feel free to watch me fight in an advanced class (multiple assailants—consider this your trigger warning, google Rachael Herron I Kick Like a Girl).

The reasons I keep working with the organization are many, but the biggest ones are these:

- I see women transformed, over and over, the way it transformed me. I went from a person who was always scared (like almost always, especially when out with my wife) to someone who still gets scared (fear is a warning system, and a good one) but who doesn't worry about it anymore. I've been trained under adrenaline, so my body knows how to fight, automatically, under that same adrenaline. I don't carry pepper spray or my keys in my fist while walking through the BART parking lot, because I prefer to keep my limbs (those excellent weapons in which I trust) free.

- The boundary-setting skills taught are amazing. I use them every single day, with friends, with family, and with strangers in the park and with the dude who thought it was appropriate to tell me that I should wear heels with my skirt this morning at the grocery store.
- **Because it helps my writing. (Selfish! But true!)**

In the Basics course, IMPACT has a "custom" fight, which is my favorite part of the class. You get to fight a past event (many women choose to fight past assaults, putting a different end on them in which they win), a future fear (waking up with an assailant in your room, or being dragged to a car), or an inner critic (that voice that tells you terrible things about yourself).

Assistants are volunteers, and assisting a full course takes up a lot of time and mental/emotional space. It's exhausting though rewarding.

And honestly, I go back time after time because of the custom fight. As I help demo them for the new students, I get to do all the fights I want, over and over. It's incredibly cathartic, and I've learned I can fight and cry at the same time, no problem.

And once? I fought my book.

I was writing *The Ones Who Matter Most.* And let me tell you: *the book was not working.* I hated everything about it. It was ugly. Misshapen. The arc was off. I didn't like the characters. I hadn't unlocked it yet, and I was beginning to despair I would.

As usual, when I hit about two-thirds of the way through a book, I was miserable.

Let's list what I hate, shall we?

I hated:

- the book
- myself
- writing in general
- the main character, Abby
- the act of sitting at the desk
- the act of first-drafting
- the act of revision
- did I mention myself? Myself!

I absolutely, one-hundred percent knew that I was a fraud. This book would be the one that showed me to everyone else as such.

The lead instructor asked me to fight an inner critic for class, to demonstrate it for the students. I ran through all the options (body image, chronic guilt, etc.) and then I rejected them all.

"Can I fight my book?"

The lead suited instructor (the guy who wears the huge padded suit that you hit and kick with full force, no holding back) said he could play that role.

So he was my book.

He circled me on the mat, starting out quietly.

"This isn't going to work."

I turned to face him.

He said, "You're a fraud. You can't write this. You suck at it. This is going to be the time that you really, truly fail."

"Stop." My voice shook.

"You really think people *like* reading what you write? They're being polite! Think of those bad reviews! Those reviewers are the only ones who are right. You suck. You're in over your head and this is the time you drown."

I raised my hands into my ready stance, making sure I was

steady on my feet. I turned to track him. "You're wrong," I managed.

"Just give up. Better keep your day job, loser, you're gonna need it. You're a terrible writer, and you're never going to get better."

"You're wrong!" I finally found my voice. "I'm a good writer. I know what I'm doing. This is my process, and I go through it every time."

"You suck."

"I'm a good writer!" I was shouting now. "I can do this! I know I can! This is my dream for a reason, and I've got this!"

"Give up. You're a *fraud!*"

The book-wearing-pads grabbed my arm and I unleashed. While delivering blows to its solar plexus, face and groin, I took it down. From a ground position, I kicked it as hard as I could, all the while yelling "No!" My voice powered each strike, making each stronger. "*No! No! You're wrong! No!*"

The suited instructors are trained not to let you off the mat until you've delivered what would be a knock-out blow in the real world.

I fought that book into the ground. I knocked it out. I kicked its everlovin' *ass*.

Then I got up, ecstatic.

I'd like to tell you that the next day I returned to the page feeling exactly the same way. I'd love to say that it was easy from then on.

That's not true. It still sucked a lot. It was hard. It required a full structural revision before the pieces started working the way I wanted them to.

But I knew this: When the critical voice started up, daily, I was able to mentally shout, "No! You're wrong!"

Then I just worked some more.

I know that my experience is unique (though do check to see

if IMPACT has a chapter near you!). Most of you won't be able to go physically kick your writing's ass, though I wish you could.

But take a minute and have a fight with it.

Act it out in the privacy of your bedroom.

Get a trusted friend to play the voice of the book (you give them the language to use, the language you will allow). DO NOT HIT THE FRIEND, PLEASE.

Or play both parts.

If this is embarrassing, write it out and do it in your mind.

You'll feel silly, for sure.

But you'll also feel better afterward.

Would you stick up for a friend who was being talked to the way your mind talks to you? You sure as hell would.

Stick up for yourself.

Duke it out.

And guess what? In this role-playing, *you always win.* The book never does. You win, even if it takes a couple (dozen) rounds.

Onward!

xo,

Rachael

CHAPTER TWENTY-FIVE

Fill Your Own Well First

Dear writers,

This week I took a day off.

It was supposed to be Monday, but Monday turned into a savagely roaring Monday, and I had to pick up my chair and whip, scaring it back into its cage, which took all damn day.

So I took Tuesday off. You know I've been thinking a lot about rest and deliberate play, and like anything else, thinking is not enough. So I did it.

I went to a yoga class. I've been meaning to get to a class for probably two years now. I do yoga at home every day, but I can never justify the two hours it means being out of the house, away from the desk, to go to a class, and *it was so good*. I accidentally went to a restorative, gentle class, which hadn't been what I wanted but ended up being what I needed. The teacher twisted us into weird and comfy poses using blocks and blankets, and then we'd just hang out in them. I almost fell asleep once (and seriously, for the next few days, I really *felt* some of the easy core work she had us do).

Then I put the top down on my wee SmartCar and headed to the coast.

At first, I was listening to some writing podcasts (my faves include The Creative Penn and The Sell More Books Show), but even before I hit the water at Ocean Beach on the far side of San Francisco, I'd switched to music. I didn't want to work even just in my mind.

I sang, instead. I sang loudly and badly and with huge gusto.

I stopped at a friend's house and had tea. We never see each other, and it felt good just to connect and talk about her kids, our jobs, and books.

Then I drove farther south, along the cliffs, watching the ocean. I went through Montara, and Half Moon Bay, ending up in Pescadero and my favorite restaurant, Duarte's. I ordered everything I wanted—no restrictions (migraine worries be damned!). I had a salty dog, with so much salt on the rim it was more like a margarita. I had a crab melt, pickles on the side.

And I had ollalieberry pie with ice cream. Oh, the heaven of ollalieberries (a Central Coast berry hybrid—I think it's a cross between a blackberry and a boysenberry, and I know it was invented at Cal Poly San Luis Obispo, my undergrad alma mater), and the way the warm pie mixes with the cold ice cream. If I had one last meal, I think it would be this one.

I ate, and I watched the waitresses serve the old ranchers who always sit in the side room (my first five books had these ranchers in them, an homage to the Duarte's men). The flirting was high and the risk was low—eighty-seven-year-old men trying to win the affections of the fifty-something waitresses, a continual song and dance that always ends in crisp dollar tips and friendly well-wishes sent to the wives as the old ranchers head back out to their pickup trucks.

Afterward, I headed to the beach. I found a completely deserted stretch of ocean, vacant as far as the eye could see. My car was the only one in the lot.

I took out my beach blanket and tromped to the edge of the continent. I lay on my side and watched the waves break vertically rather than horizontally, asking myself why I'd never thought to watch the waves from that vantage before (it's rather spectacular). I built a very bad sandcastle. I skipped rocks (I RULE AT SKIPPING ROCKS). I climbed into a driftwood fort and imagined I could live in it forever.

Then I put on more music and drove the long way home, stuck in traffic for an extra hour.

It was worth it.

When I got home, my heart was light. I'd had a mini-retreat, all by myself, carved from 8 hours on a day I'd normally be strapped to my desk.

And the rest of the work week? My fingers flew. I got *so much done*.

The well was full.

How will you fill yours?

Just like the oxygen masks on the airplane, you can't fill the well of others with your writing until you've filled your own first.

Go out there and grab some gorgeous life, and pie, and beauty, and wild, fresh air. Suck it down, and then help yourself to more.

(Then tell me about it, if you want to. I always love hearing what you're up to.)

Onward!

xo,

Rachael

CHAPTER TWENTY-SIX

Share Your Work

Hello writers,

Sometimes I just totally forget to act like a writer.

I was at the Bay Area Book Festival today, in the RWA booth. I spent a couple of hours ostensibly "helping," but mostly that meant chatting with my fellow writers and greeting people who wandered up to our booth to talk about romance. It was a super easy gig, and it was fun.

And it was made even easier because I, um, kind of forgot to work while I was there.

I didn't bring books to sell.

I didn't publicize on social media that I'd be there so that readers could say hi if they wanted to.

I forgot to bring bookmarks.

I even forgot to bring *business cards*, something I always have on me when I have my purse, but I launched myself out of the house with just my phone and keys.

I do that sometimes. I forget.

Or really, I "forget."

You know what I mean. **It's just easier not to do something, so you kind of fail to think about it.**

It's hard work to sell books, but it's part of my job. Carissa ribbed me gently about it, and I laughed, but she was right. I *should* have thought about it.

I need to promote my work—it's part of what I do.

It's just that promo is hard, nerve-wracking, sometimes embarrassing work. *Here, I made something. Can I tell you about it?*

Sometimes I'd rather punch myself in the eye than tell people about the things that I make, about the books that I'm so inordinately proud of yet hide at the same time.

But I saw a bunch of people today being brave, telling everyone who passed their booths what their books were about. They were proud. They'd done a lot of work, and in front of them were the gorgeous, wordy fruits of their labor.

I was proud of them, and I was ashamed of myself. Now, I'm not going to cry myself to sleep tonight, don't worry. The sting was only momentary, and I'm over it now.

It was a good reminder, though.

I'm a writer, and that's not only when I'm in my office writing. It's not just when I'm with friends talking about the industry. It's not just when I'm recording my podcasts or when I'm teaching or coaching.

It's all the time.

That includes when I *literally sign myself up* to be in a place ripe for promotion.

lifts right hand I solemnly swear I'll take the opportunities I'm given for being proud of my work, for giving other people the chance to read my words.

This week, on my podcast, I talked to Monica Leonelle, who said something truly inspiring. She said when she gets bogged down in the "I suck at writing" thinking, she takes a step back and thinks about the people she's helping by doing her work.

Your work, no matter what it is, can and *will* help someone.

Don't hold yourself back from sharing that help.

My dearest wish, when it comes to my novels, is that they help someone get through something hard in their lives. I've been lucky enough to hear sometimes that I've accomplished that, and hot damn, that's one of the best feelings in the world.

I promise I'll be more open to sharing what I have to offer.

Will you do the same?

Onward!

xo,

Rachael

CHAPTER TWENTY-SEVEN

Sailing, On and Off the Page

Hi writers,

I've mentioned before my penchant for doing things that scare me.

It's not ideal. What it means is that I get a wild hair to do something new, something that deep down I desperately want to do and at the same time wish I would never have to face. It leads to some misery and upset stomach and me muttering wildly at myself in the car, "What am I doing? *Why* am I doing this? I hate this idea so much! I want to go home!"

Then I do the scary thing and most of the time, I love it (not always—I will regret my one day of Krav Maga for the rest of my life).

I don't always do things quickly (this is more surprising to me than anyone else). I got a yen to learn to sail five years ago. I planned to learn to sail during my fortieth year, and now I'm forty-four, and I only learned this last weekend.

I grew up in and around boats. We were always near the water. Dad always had small sailboats, the kind you could strap to the roof of a car. I distinctly remember one made of styrofoam which I would pick away at with my fingers, unable to resist the lure of the snap-crunch of the foam crumbling away. I also distinctly remember the time that boat sank off the Marin coast. Mom and my sisters watched as three burly youths barreled into the water to save him—all four came in laughing, dragging pieces of the boat with them. My poor water-phobic mother was not pleased. I tried not to think about all the styrofoam I'd pulled off.

But even though I spent hours and hours in his hand-hewn wooden boats (bailing, or watching for rocks), I never caught the bug. I was content to sit on the side of the bigger sailboats I've been on as an adult. I steered a sailboat under the Golden Gate Bridge once because the captain dared me to (and it was cool, I'll admit that). But apart from that mild yearning, I ignored the pull to the water.

This last trip to Venice cemented this for me: I am most happy when on the water. My sister Bethany is happy driving. I just want to be bobbing up and down in something that could sink. My brain loves the feeling.

This past weekend, I spent the weekend on the water at Lake Merritt in Oakland, a great place to learn to sail because the winds are strong and capricious. I took a cheap three-day class through Oakland Parks and Rec and while I'm only two days into it, I've finally caught the bug, my father will be happy to know.

First, we learned things while sitting in a classroom. Nothing (not *one* thing) made sense to me. I was concerned about the outhaul and the boomvang and cunningham because if a boat was outfitted with such important yet silly-sounding things, how could I be trusted to remember to install/tighten/hitch them properly? My hands, so clever with string and yarn, rebelled at learning to make a bowline (pronounced BOW-lun because these people don't talk right. Leeward is pronounced loo-erd. I'm capsizing is pronounced holy-fucking-shit-help).

But then we got out on the eight-foot one-person El Toros.

We rigged them and sailed on the lake on a long line so that when we got into trouble, the instructor could tow us back. I was ***not*** the first person to capsize.

The second day, yesterday, we rigged our fourteen-foot Catalinas. They seemed huge compared to the El Toros, but the thing was: everything was the same.

The mainsail worked the same way.

The tiller worked the same way.

The principles were all the same.

I realized I'd learned the basics of sailing in a day and a half, and this was brought home to me when I saw a Moana GIF—I understood what she was doing on the boat.

Boats, with all their lines and rigging and flappety-flaps and eccentric wobbles, had always been mysterious to me.

But after breaking it into bite-sized, manageable pieces of knowledge, I get how sailing works.

I'm by no means *good* at it. In winds of thirty mph (twenty-eight knots, officially small-craft advisory weather), I sailed the boat into a place I couldn't come back from and the instructor had to tow me out (the tow of shame). I fell off the boat leaping for the dock, catching myself on the edge of the dock with a yoga-like barrel roll that kept me out of the water but has me covered in livid purple bruises today. I still don't have any idea what to do when I'm stuck in irons (it's called patience, and I'm not sure where to buy more of that).

I know the basics, though. And those don't change. Practice and lessons and more practice will help me become better and more accomplished and less anxious. But I know the *how* and the *why* and I know I can do the thing to make the boat fly (it *is* flying, with lift and drag and all—I had no idea!).

It's the same with writing.

It's terrifying. You want to do it, but you're afraid you'll capsize, or get lost, or hurt yourself.

But you keep getting drawn back to it.

Your whole life, you've been drawn to blank notebooks and new pens, looking for the way in.

Here's the thing: **You already have the way in.**

- In sailing, you steer with a rudder while you manipulate the shape of the mainsail. Those are the basics of sailing.
- In knitting, you knit and you purl. Those are the basics for garments.
- In writing, you think of words and set them on paper/screen. Those are the basics for books.

You think of words.

You set them down.

That's it.

Sure, that's easy. And yes, it's also incredibly complicated and so much more than that. But you, my friend, have cracked the basic code. *SO* many people look at writers longingly and say, "I have a story. I wish I could do that."

It comes down to this: It's simple. It's not rocket science. Boats sail by catching the wind. Words are written one at a time, as the author thinks of them.

That's all.

It takes bravery, though, I know that.

And you have that.

Onward!

xo,

Rachael

CHAPTER TWENTY-EIGHT

Disappointment Served with a Side of Relief

Hi writers,

Today on Twitter I tweeted mysteriously about a hope balloon that popped. I can't do the tell-all thing on the socials, but I'll tell *you*, of course.

Here's the straight dirt: a major editor at a publisher I'd love to work for solicited the thriller I'm writing.

So I polished the opening. My agent submitted it. I sat on my hands when I wasn't chewing on my nails, and we waited a while.

Today we heard that the editor is leaving the publishing house to go freelance, thus orphaning any hopes I had of them coddling, raising, and nurturing my small, scary thriller baby.

But here's the thing: it isn't sucking *that* much.

I'm slightly relieved, which I would not have predicted I would be this morning.

See, while the proposal and sample chapters had been out there, I hadn't been able to work on the book.

It doesn't make any sense. There was literally nothing keeping me from moving forward into the last quarter of the unfinished manuscript. I *should* have been moving forward. That's what I would have advised *you* to do.

But I couldn't. There was something in me that said, "What if they fall in love with the *idea* of this book, but instead of it being a rapey/murdery thriller, they'd like it to be a small, Skittle-flavored* children's book about puppies? If I finish the scary thriller, then I'll just have to Skittle it all up! The less I do now the better."

So I was stuck.

Sure, I've been busy working on other things, but I've been feeling my wheels spin a bit. I want to be pushing the words around, bossing them into standing over there and looking more multisyllabic than they really are.

Now, come this Monday, I get to do that.

I get to open the Scrivener file and race through my synopsis. I get to skim all the chapters to make sure all those words I loved and abandoned are still there.

And then: I get to *write*.

I literally can't wait. (Okay, literally in the figurative sense because it's Friday night and I'm going sailing again tomorrow and I need to study my boating test so I can get all certified and stuff.)

May all your disappointments be small, your winds fair, and your words many and lovely.

Onward!

xo,

Rachael

PS—I'm aware Skittle isn't a flavor, but it kind of is when you think of how it tastes when you eat eleven at a time, which is what I might do tonight, repeatedly, because even though I'm bouncy and feeling very publishing-resilient I still have a few feelings that are ruffled and showing off various shades of bruise-green tenderness. Also, I may have asked the wife to pick up some Scotch on her way home. But really, that's just me using something I would normally be very disappointed over to make her run errands for me. Don't tell. She's also going to have to watch *Four Weddings and a Funeral*, because I'm shameless about my pout lip.

CHAPTER TWENTY-NINE

I Found My Mother

Hi y'all,

I made the most astonishing discovery yesterday. It's like a dream come true, and literally, it *was* a dream come true. I'd dreamed very vividly the night before about my mother. She was with my friend Sophie's mother, and they told us they loved us. It was so startlingly vibrant and intense that I emailed Sophie about it as soon as I woke up. It wasn't a normal I-was-eating-pickles-at-the-carnival-then-I-was-in-a-garden-with-my-high-school-English-teacher kind of dream. It felt real.

Sophie and I had lunch a few hours later. We talked more about the dream.

Then I went home and in a full-blown fit of writing procrastination, I started mucking out the front porch which routinely becomes our dumping ground for boxes of clothes and books to donate, packages we haven't bothered to open yet (new kayak paddles, the cable box the internet company sent us that we've never hooked up), dog food bags, and all the stuff we just don't know what to do with.

It's embarrassing. It's our "garage" as we have no garage and very few and tiny closets. Guests have to walk through the hell of it to get inside our nice house. It smells like cats (they sleep there at night and every once in while they decide they hate the cat box —gah.) Once a year or so I spring clean it, and yesterday was the day.

Now, a couple of years ago, I cleaned out my office. I KonMari'd it, getting rid of SO MUCH crap. I also put all the stuff I mean to digitize into cardboard boxes and put them on the porch. The boxes held old photographs, all my old writings, and my mother's photos and writings.

Yep, my mother was a writer, too.

If you've followed my work at all, you already know that she was pivotal to me and who I am now. My mom and I were really, really close. I considered her one of my very best friends and biggest champions. One of the biggest regrets of my life is not sharing my first completed novel (which went on to be my first published book) with her, but honestly, she was too sick then, and pushing it on her would have been the wrong thing to do. I just really wish she had read it, that's all.

But as a writer herself, my mother remained as carefully in control of her emotions as she did in every other part of her life. One of her friends once told me, "You know, your mom is my best friend. But I don't know her at *all.*"

Oh, yeah. That was my mom. She could deflect attention like she was wearing conversational armor. A primary goal of my whole life was to get her to tell me things about her past. She never wanted to speak of any of it, and not because she'd had a bad youth - she hadn't. She'd had a delightful one, for the most part. She was just so *private*. (The apple fell really far from the tree on this one.)

In the articles that she sold to magazines and newspapers, she always wrote *about* other things. An old-school journalist, she kept her personality out of her work.

When I inherited her writings, I combed through them, looking for something more personal. I found an essay about her being pregnant with me. It was short but lovely. That was it. Everything else was impersonal and left me craving *more*.

Yesterday, as I was finally taking back the porch, I found the boxes I'd piled there. Time to move them to new digs! (Not to digitize them yet, oh, no. That would be too much work. Time to move them out of cardboard boxes and into more protective plastic ones which could then be stored in our bedroom closet! More procrastination, ahoy!)

So I paged through Mom's writing again, for at least the third or fourth time. I found book review after boring book review. Articles on gardening. Birds.

I dropped them all in the clear plastic bin. I lifted the sharpie to write on the outside: *Jan's papers.*

And I looked through the bin, to the top folder. It said clearly, *The Morning Pages.*

My brain stalled.

My mother. And Morning Pages?

Impossible.

Now, any of you who were pursuing creativity in the 1990s remember the Morning Pages. They were a tool in Julia Cameron's book, *The Artist's Way*. Basically, whether you're a writer or not, you start your day with three handwritten pages, and you do this for twelve weeks. You don't think about what you're writing; you just blab. The words come from the bottom of your soul and the top of your mind. You don't worry about grammar or spelling. You don't reread. You can write "I don't know what to write" for three pages, and that totally counts. (I still recommend the book. Grab it if you've never done it.)

I popped open the box and yanked out the file folder. It was orange and had black printing on front: *THERE IS NO ANTIDOTE FOR TERROR.*

Inside were 217 pages of morning pages in my mother's hand.

I flipped forward. I read a few lines. Yes. These were hers. Really, really hers.

They were from 1996.

I was still living at home then, finishing college and about to leave home for grad school (I was a mama's girl and never really wanted to leave). I know that I'd started morning pages the year before (and kept them going for years), and I have a vague memory of encouraging her to do the Artist's Way. I also remember hearing her complain she had nothing to write about, and I remember saying, "No one does. Just write anyway."

So yesterday, I set the folder to the side. (I'm one of those people who always save the best for last.)

I finished my five-hour clean-out. I scrubbed the front porch. I drove to the thrift store with my SmartCar full-to-bulging. I bought some wine and some salt and vinegar potato chips.

I went home and took the chips, the folder, and a glass of wine onto the back porch.

Then I read.

And I found my mother.

I found *her.* This voice—the one on the page—was the one I heard when she'd had two glasses of wine (one past her giggle limit). This voice was the one I heard in a little *osteria* in Venice as she told me just the barest bit about her childhood home. This voice was the one I heard on a dark road in New Zealand, lit only by glowworms, as she talked a tiny bit about an old boyfriend.

It was the voice I'd always wanted to hear.

She wrote about her childhood bedroom. About her first attempts at making art (age seven: she diverted a creek to make islands, and covered them with flowers). About her subsequent attempts, tracking them through her life.

She wrote about us. About my sister Beth and her baths. About Christy and her artistic talents. About going to a writer's reading with me (oooh, she did *not* like that one poet).

She wrote about her cats. She wrote about her garden and

where her love of each scent came from. I learned amaryllis would always remind her of her father's funeral. That violet was the best scent of all.

And this: I learned that she felt she was locked down by inertia. Her most-frequently used affirmation in the pages (affirmations are strongly encouraged by Julia Cameron) is **"I can overcome inertia."**

This is *wild.* My mother was like me—we never, ever stop moving. We're always, always doing *something*, every minute of the day. But she really felt that her creativity was stuck and that it was inertia that held her there.

She would never have said this to anyone. This was a deep feeling, and (as she confesses in the pages), she couldn't speak these kinds of things. She went mum when it came to emotions or relationship issues, her tongue tied.

But lord, she gets it on the page.

And funny! I'd almost forgotten how *funny* she was. She was the smartest person I've ever known, and I knew that, but I'd forgotten her sharp wit, always ready to tease, sometimes a tiny bit too hard (something I can also be prone to doing).

I do, I promise, have a point in telling you this.

Leave something behind.

Oh, god, Rachael, you had to go to the macabre, didn't you?

Yes, I did.

This is one of the biggest gifts I will ever, ever receive. Last night, on the solstice (which she always loved and honored), I read on the porch until the light faded from the sky and the frogs in the creek became deafening.

I sat with my mother and heard her for the first time since she died almost exactly nine years ago.

I was *with* her. I was much too happy to be sad.

If you have a writing bone in your body, do this: Leave something behind. Write in a journal, even if it's only every once in a while. Don't write about the Things You Got Done; no one cares about a list. Write about how they made you feel. Be honest. I'm only fifty-five pages into my mother's pages, and I'm hoping desperately she says something *agonizing* about me (she hasn't yet). Oh, to hear her despair of me ever doing anything with my life (I showed very little promise for a very long time).

I'm only a quarter of the way through, and I'm going to try to take my time with them. Then I'm going to transcribe them so I can share them with family (her handwriting is easy for me to read and very hard for most people including other family members).

I just can't believe I'd never found them before. I'd *looked.*

I have a very strong feeling she saved them for me, for now. For the solstice of the year that I would be strong enough to have nothing but joy in my heart as I read.

Leave something behind for the ones who love you so they can truly commune with you later, so they can hear your specific and wonderful voice. Tell them what you think. Be *you*. Be true. Be broken and fallible and honest and *you.*

You're amazing. I know you're (probably) not planning on leaving the earth anytime soon, but even if you are, first, you are loved, and second, there's still time.

Put your heart in a bottle and throw it in the ocean of time. Someone you love will want to find you someday. I promise.

Thanks for reading.

Love,

Rachael

WHAT TO READ NEXT

Do you want to get out of your own way and get the words on the page? Grab *Fast-Draft Your Memoir* which *sounds* like it's just about memoir, but it isn't. It's everything Rachael knows about writing (fast-drafting! revision! confidence!), all in one place.

Grab it now, wherever books are sold.

ABOUT RACHAEL HERRON

Don't miss another email of encouragement for your writing! Sign up for Rachael's mailing list and get your free Stop Stalling and Write PDF: Go to RachaelHerron.com/Write

Rachael Herron is the bestselling author of the novel *The Ones Who Matter Most* (named an Editor's Pick by Library Journal), as well as more than twenty other novels and memoirs. Her latest non-fiction is *Fast-Draft Your Memoir: Write Your Life Story in 45 Hours*. She received her MFA in writing from Mills College, Oakland and she teaches writing in the extension programs at both UC Berkeley and Stanford. She's proud to be a New Zealander as well as a US citizen, though her Kiwi accent only comes out when she's very tired. She's honored to be a member of the NaNoWriMo Writers Board.

EXCERPT

Excerpt from Chapter Thirteen of Fast-Draft Your Memoir

13. Finally, Time to Write!

Yes! It's time!

And look. I have every single bit of confidence in you. I've had many students gaze at me with the same deer-in-the-headlights expression that you're giving me now, and they finished their memoirs even though they never thought they could.

You're going to, also.

Make that decision right now. This isn't an "I hope I can do this" situation. This is an "I'm going to write and *finish* my memoir" state of affairs.

You're going to do this.

The next question I always get is "*How* the frak am I supposed to do this?"

You're going to write this book scene by scene. That's all.

Each of the scenes in your book will fit into one of those four structural boxes we talked about in the last chapter.

But you might not actually know where those scenes fit yet. That's okay.

You do *not* have to write in chronological order. You can write scenes from your outline in any order at all. Write what excites you. If you can't wait to write that summer vacation morning memory, write it now. Move toward what you *want* to write. You don't have to start at the beginning. You can write scenes and throw them into a virtual bin in the middle of the floor and sort them into their appropriate boxes later. You'll be able to look at each scene and ask yourself, "was I reacting at this point? Or was I the actor in my own life, making my own decisions? Does this particular bit belong in Act Two or Act Three?" But you decide those things later. For now, you're just writing a crappy first draft that you can fix later. If you winced at that, start trying to accept crappiness. Personally, I find it useful to challenge myself to write *truly* terribly. At least then I have a goal I can strive for, and it works—I get my words done, and they're always, always fixable. Yours will be, too.

However, many people (including myself) are linear writers and don't want to write out of order. We like to start at the beginning and write through to the end. That's fine, too, just know that you don't have to stick to it. I get pretty rigid myself, both in fiction and memoir, and I shove myself through scenes like I'm trying to fit a jar of peanut butter into a thimble. *I will get there if it kills me.* This can be unpleasant, but it's my way. You'll find your way as you go.

Here's a bit of advice to help you get there.

THE BEGINNING

1. Have a word-count goal and write it on your calendar for the week. Don't write out your word count goal for the whole book, because I guarantee you'll miss a week's goal, and then you'll have to rejigger your whole calendar for a month or more (ask me how I know). But if you have three hours free for writing this week, and if you think you can get three thousand words written in that time, plan it. On Sunday morning, you'll write a thousand. Tuesday night, five hundred. Thursday, another five hundred. Friday morning, the last thousand. Write it down, then when the time rolls around, *write.*

2. Celebrate that first day of writing! You will feel elated, guaranteed. Huzzah! You did it! You've started something *huge!* If you drink, have a glass of champagne. If you don't, eat your favorite dessert. Toast yourself and your supreme daring. You're amazing! You're a writer! (You're a writer if you're writing. That's how it works. Claim that.)

3. Know that the next time you sit down, it *might* not feel as great as it did the first day. The high does wear off, and writing becomes more painful the further we go into a piece of work. That's okay, and it's totally normal. I often liken it to exercise (gah)—it sucks to work out, but it always feels good later.

4. Your voice is your voice is your voice. You'll have days when you *know* in your very bones that you're the very worst writer who ever lived. A caveman scratching symbols on a wall in charcoal is a better writer than you are. And then you'll have days when your writing is miraculous. Your words could convert a Catholic nun to Satanism. Your sentences leap off the page and build castles around your ears. The astonishing thing is this: when you go back to revise (later!), you won't be able to tell which were the days you wrote "well" or "badly." Your voice is your voice. The way we feel about our writing changes just like our moods. Don't trust your moods. Just keep showing up, day after day.

5. After you've begun, it's normal to feel that you'll never finish. It's such a herculean effort just to write one scene, how are you ever going to write the whole book? It's an impossible task. You can't do this.

Yes, you can.

Yes, you will.

One scene at a time. Or even just one paragraph at a time. Many short writing sessions add up to a finished book. You're on the way.

THE MIDDLE

1. The middle part might be difficult. Wait. It *will* be. Often called "the sagging middle," this is common. I call a first draft the "who cares" draft because it's easy, when stuck in the middle, to think that nobody cares. Your mom doesn't care. Your husband is sick of hearing about it. Your kids roll their eyes.

Worst of all, *you* stop caring.

It's hard work. Who's going to want to read all this crap? No one, that's who. Might as well quit before I waste any more time on this stupid endeavor.

Normal! That's so, so normal. No one cares, not even you.

That changes—you'll just have to trust me on this. You'll find your mojo again, and when you're revising (later!), you'll *love* the book again. Accept that you might not love it while writing it.

BUY NOW to continue reading the full book!

Made in the USA
San Bernardino, CA
22 November 2019